Xamarin 4.x Cross-Platform Application Development

Third Edition

Develop powerful cross-platform applications with Xamarin

Jonathan Peppers

BIRMINGHAM - MUMBAI

Xamarin 4.x Cross-Platform Application Development

Third Edition

First published: February 2014

Second edition: February 2015

Third edition: December 2016

Production reference: 1221216

Published by Packt Publishing Ltd.
Livery Place
35 Livery Street
Birmingham
B3 2PB, UK.
ISBN 978-1-78646-541-2

www.packtpub.com

Credits

Author

Jonathan Peppers

Reviewer

Esteban Solano Granados

Commissioning Editor

Ashwin Nair

Acquisition Editor

Reshma Raman

Content Development Editor

Narendrakumar Tripathi

Technical Editor

Anushree Arun Tendulkar

Copy Editor

Safis Editing

Project Coordinator

Devanshi Doshi

Proofreader

Safis Editing

Indexer

Tejal Daruwale Soni

Graphics

Jason Monteiro

Production Coordinator

Aparna Bhagat

About the Author

Jonathan Peppers is a Xamarin MVP and lead developer on popular apps and games at Hitcents such as the Hanx Writer (for Tom Hanks) and the Draw a Stickman franchise. Jon has been working with C# for over 10 years working on a wide range of projects at Hitcents. Jon began his career working Self-Checkout software written in WinForms and later migrated to WPF. Over his career, he has worked with many .NET-centric technologies such as ASP.Net WebForms, MVC, Windows Azure, WinRT/UWP, F#, and Unity3D.

In recent years, Hitcents has been heavily investing in mobile development with Xamarin, and has development over 50 mobile applications across multiple platforms.

I would like to thank my wife, Amy Kate, and my son, Levi, for giving me the free time to write this book. You are both my inspiration and "why I do what I do".

About the Reviewer

Esteban Solano Granados is a senior software engineer, Microsoft and Xamarin MVP from Cartago, Costa Rica and he enjoys learning, talk, and help others to learn about software development for the web and mobile by using his knowledge of JavaScript and C# with Xamarin, Asp.Net, NodeJS and other technologies.

www.PacktPub.com

For support files and downloads related to your book, please visit www.PacktPub.com.

Did you know that Packt offers eBook versions of every book published, with PDF and ePub files available? You can upgrade to the eBook version at www.PacktPub.com and as a print book customer, you are entitled to a discount on the eBook copy. Get in touch with us at service@packtpub.com for more details.

At www.PacktPub.com, you can also read a collection of free technical articles, sign up for a range of free newsletters and receive exclusive discounts and offers on Packt books and eBooks.

https://www.packtpub.com/mapt

Get the most in-demand software skills with Mapt. Mapt gives you full access to all Packt books and video courses, as well as industry-leading tools to help you plan your personal development and advance your career.

Why subscribe?

- Fully searchable across every book published by Packt
- Copy and paste, print, and bookmark content
- On demand and accessible via a web browser

Customer Feedback

Thank you for purchasing this Packt book. We take our commitment to improving our content and products to meet your needs seriously—that's why your feedback is so valuable. Whatever your feelings about your purchase, please consider leaving a review on this book's Amazon page. Not only will this help us, more importantly it will also help others in the community to make an informed decision about the resources that they invest in to learn.

You can also review for us on a regular basis by joining our reviewers' club. **If you're interested in joining, or would like to learn more about the benefits we offer, please contact us**: customerreviews@packtpub.com

Table of Contents

Preface

Xamarin has built great products for developing iOS and Android applications in C#: Xamarin Studio, an addin for Visual Studio, Xamarin.iOS, and Xamarin.Android. Xamarin gives you direct access to the native APIs on each platform and the flexibility of sharing C# code. Using Xamarin and C#, you get better productivity when compared to Java or Objective-C, and still retain great performance compared to an HTML or JavaScript solution.

In this book, we will develop a real-world sample application to demonstrate what you can do with Xamarin technologies, and build on core platform concepts for iOS and Android. We will also cover advanced topics such as push notifications, retrieving contacts, using the camera, and GPS location. With Xamarin 3, a new framework was introduced called Xamarin.Forms. We will cover the basics of Xamarin.Forms and how you can apply it to cross-platform development. Finally, we will walkthrough what it takes to submit your application to the Apple App Store and Google Play.

What this book covers

Chapter 1, *Xamarin Setup*, is a guide for installing the appropriate Xamarin software and native SDKs for doing cross-platform development. Directs Windows users on how to connect to a Mac on their local network for doing iOS development in Visual Studio.

Chapter 2, *Hello, Platforms!*, is a walkthrough of creating a simple calculator application on iOS and Android, which also covers some basic concepts on each platform.

Chapter 3, *Code Sharing between iOS and Android*, is an introduction of code sharing techniques and project setup strategies that can be used with Xamarin.

Chapter 4, *XamSnap - A Cross-Platform App*, is an introduction to a sample application we will be building throughout the book. In this chapter we will write all the shared code for the application complete with unit tests.

Chapter 5, *XamSnap for iOS*, shows us how to implement the iOS user interface for XamSnap and cover various iOS development concepts.

Chapter 6, *XamSnap for Android*, shows us how to implement the Android version of XamSnap and introduce Android-specific development concepts.

Chapter 7, *Deploying and Testing on Devices*, is a walkthrough the painful process of deploying your first application to a device. We also cover why it is important to always test your application on real devices.

Chapter 8, *Contacts, Camera, and Location*, introduces the library, Xamarin.Mobile, as a cross-platform way to access users' contacts, camera, and GPS location and add these features to our XamSnap application.

Chapter 9, *Web Services with Push Notifications*, shows us how to implement a real backend web service for XamSnap using Windows Azure leveraging Azure Functions and Azure Notification Hubs.

Chapter 10, *Third-Party Libraries*, covers the various options of using third party libraries with Xamarin and how you can even leverage native Java and Objective-C libraries.

Chapter 11, *Xamarin.Forms*, helps us discover Xamarin's latest framework, Xamarin.Forms, and how you can leverage it to build cross-platform applications.

Chapter 12, *App Store Submission*, will walk us through the process of submitting your app to the Apple App Store and Google Play.

What you need for this book

For this book you will need a Mac computer running at least OS X 10.10. Apple requires iOS applications to be compiled on a Mac, so Xamarin has the same requirement. You can either use Xamarin Studio (best for Mac) or Visual Studio (best for Windows) as an IDE. Developers on Windows can work on iOS applications in Visual Studio by connecting to a Mac on their local network. Visit https://xamarin.com/download or https://visualstudio.com/download to download the appropriate software.

Who this book is for

This book is for developers that are already familiar with C# and want to learn mobile development with Xamarin. If you have worked in ASP.NET, WPF, WinRT, Windows Phone, or UWP, then you will be right at home using this book to develop native iOS and Android applications.

Conventions

In this book, you will find a number of text styles that distinguish between different kinds of information. Here are some examples of these styles and an explanation of their meaning.

Code words in text, database table names, folder names, filenames, file extensions, pathnames, dummy URLs, user input, and Twitter handles are shown as follows: "run asynchronous code in C# using the `await` keyword."

A block of code is set as follows:

```
class ChuckNorris
{
    void DropKick()
    {
        Console.WriteLine("Dropkick!");
    }
}
```

When we wish to draw your attention to a particular part of a code block, the relevant lines or items are set in bold:

```
class ChuckNorris
{
    void DropKick()
    {
        Console.WriteLine("Dropkick!");
    }
}
```

Any command-line input or output is written as follows:

```
# xbuild MyProject.csproj
```

New terms and **important words** are shown in bold. Words that you see on the screen, for example, in menus or dialog boxes, appear in the text like this: "In order to download new modules, we will go to **Files** | **Settings** | **Project Name** | **Project Interpreter**."

 Warnings or important notes appear in a box like this.

Tips and tricks appear like this.

Reader feedback

Feedback from our readers is always welcome. Let us know what you think about this book-what you liked or disliked. Reader feedback is important for us as it helps us develop titles that you will really get the most out of. To send us general feedback, simply e-mail feedback@packtpub.com, and mention the book's title in the subject of your message. If there is a topic that you have expertise in and you are interested in either writing or contributing to a book, see our author guide at www.packtpub.com/authors.

Customer support

Now that you are the proud owner of a Packt book, we have a number of things to help you to get the most from your purchase.

Downloading the example code

You can download the example code files for this book from your account at http://www.p acktpub.com. If you purchased this book elsewhere, you can visit http://www.packtpub.c om/support and register to have the files e-mailed directly to you.

You can download the code files by following these steps:

1. Log in or register to our website using your e-mail address and password.
2. Hover the mouse pointer on the **SUPPORT** tab at the top.
3. Click on **Code Downloads & Errata**.
4. Enter the name of the book in the **Search** box.
5. Select the book for which you're looking to download the code files.
6. Choose from the drop-down menu where you purchased this book from.
7. Click on **Code Download**.

Once the file is downloaded, please make sure that you unzip or extract the folder using the latest version of:

- WinRAR / 7-Zip for Windows
- Zipeg / iZip / UnRarX for Mac
- 7-Zip / PeaZip for Linux

The code bundle for the book is also hosted on GitHub at `https://github.com/PacktPubl ishing/Xamarin4x-Cross-Platform-Application-Development-Third-Edition`. We also have other code bundles from our rich catalog of books and videos available at `https://gi thub.com/PacktPublishing/`. Check them out!

Downloading the color images of this book

We also provide you with a PDF file that has color images of the screenshots/diagrams used in this book. The color images will help you better understand the changes in the output. You can download this file from `https://www.packtpub.com/sites/default/files/down loads/Xamarin4xCrossPlatformApplicationDevelopmentThirdEdition_ColorImages.p df`.

Errata

Although we have taken every care to ensure the accuracy of our content, mistakes do happen. If you find a mistake in one of our books-maybe a mistake in the text or the code-we would be grateful if you could report this to us. By doing so, you can save other readers from frustration and help us improve subsequent versions of this book. If you find any errata, please report them by visiting `http://www.packtpub.com/submit-errata`, selecting your book, clicking on the **Errata Submission Form** link, and entering the details of your errata. Once your errata are verified, your submission will be accepted and the errata will be uploaded to our website or added to any list of existing errata under the Errata section of that title.

To view the previously submitted errata, go to `https://www.packtpub.com/books/conten t/support` and enter the name of the book in the search field. The required information will appear under the **Errata** section.

Piracy

Piracy of copyrighted material on the Internet is an ongoing problem across all media. At Packt, we take the protection of our copyright and licenses very seriously. If you come across any illegal copies of our works in any form on the Internet, please provide us with the location address or website name immediately so that we can pursue a remedy.

Please contact us at `copyright@packtpub.com` with a link to the suspected pirated material.

We appreciate your help in protecting our authors and our ability to bring you valuable content.

Questions

If you have a problem with any aspect of this book, you can contact us at `questions@packtpub.com`, and we will do our best to address the problem.

1
Xamarin Setup

If you are reading this book, you probably already have a deep love for C#, .NET, and tools like Microsoft Visual Studio. Mobile development with the native SDKs seems daunting when you think about the work of learning a new platform, a new IDE, new application models, and perhaps a programming language or two. Xamarin aims to delight .NET developers with the tools for developing native iOS, Android, and Mac applications in C#.

There are many advantages of choosing Xamarin to develop mobile applications instead of Java on Android and Objective-C/Swift on iOS. You can share code between both of these platforms and you can be more productive by taking advantage of the advanced language features of C# and the .NET base class libraries. Alternatively, you would have to write an entire application, twice, for both Android and iOS.

In comparison with other techniques for developing cross-platform applications with JavaScript and HTML, Xamarin has some distinct advantages. C# is generally more performant than JavaScript, and Xamarin gives developers direct access to the native APIs on each platform. This allows Xamarin applications to have a native look and perform in a manner similar to their Java or Objective-C counterparts. Xamarin's tooling works by compiling your C# into a native ARM executable that can be packaged as an iOS or Android application. It bundles a stripped-down version of the Mono runtime with your application that only includes the features of the base class libraries your app uses.

In this chapter, we'll set up everything you need to get started on developing with Xamarin. By the end of this chapter, we'll have all the proper SDKs and tools installed, and all the developer accounts needed for app-store submission.

In this chapter, we will cover:

- An introduction to Xamarin tools and technology
- Installing Xcode, Apple's IDE
- Setting up all Xamarin tools and software
- Connecting Visual Studio to a Mac
- Setting up the Android emulator
- Enrolling in the iOS developer program
- Registering for Google Play

Understanding Xamarin

Xamarin has developed three core products for developing cross-platform applications: **Xamarin Studio**, **Xamarin.iOS**, and **Xamarin.Android**. Xamarin Studio is a C# IDE, while **Xamarin.iOS** and **Xamarin.Android** are the core tooling that enable C# applications to run on iOS and Android, respectively. These tools allow developers to leverage the native libraries on iOS and Android, and are built on the Mono runtime.

Mono, an open source implementation of C# and the .NET framework, was originally developed by Novell to be used on Linux operating systems. Since iOS and Android are similarly based on Linux, Novell was able to develop MonoTouch and Mono for Android as products to target the new mobile platforms. Shortly after their release, a larger company acquired Novell, and the Mono team left to form a new company aimed primarily at mobile development. Xamarin was founded to focus on these tools for developing with C# on iOS and Android.

Getting a development machine ready for cross-platform application development can take some time. And to make matters worse, Apple and Google both have their own requirements for development on their respective platforms. If you plan on developing on Windows with Visual Studio, your setup will be a bit different than on Mac OS X. Keep in mind that iOS development on Windows requires a Mac on your local network. Let's go over what needs to be installed on your machine.

The building blocks for Xamarin development on Mac OS X are as follows:

- **Xcode**: Apple's core IDE for developing iOS and Mac applications in Objective-C
- **The Mono runtime for Mac**: This is required for compiling and running C# programs on OS X
- **Java**: This is the core runtime for running Java applications on OS X
- **Android SDK**: This contains Google's standard SDK, device drivers, and emulators for native Android development
- **Xamarin.iOS**: This is Xamarin's core product for iOS development
- **Xamarin.Android**: This is Xamarin's core product for Android development

The required software for Xamarin development on Windows are as follows:

- **Visual Studio or Xamarin Studio**: Either IDE will work for Xamarin development on Windows.
- **.NET Framework 4.5 or later**: This comes with Visual Studio or recent versions of Windows.
- **Java**: This is the core runtime for running Java applications on Windows.
- **Android SDK**: This contains Google's standard SDK, device drivers, and emulators for native Android development.
- **A Mac on your local network set up for Xamarin.iOS development**: Apple requires iOS development to be done on OS X as part of their licensing agreement. A Mac will need to be set up for Xamarin.iOS development as listed above.
- **Xamarin for Windows**: This is Xamarin's core product for Windows; it includes both Xamarin.Android and Xamarin.iOS.

Each of these will take some time to download and install. If you can access a fast Internet connection, it will help speed up the installation and setup process. With everything ready to go, let's move ahead step by step and, hopefully, we can skip a few dead ends you might otherwise run into.

Installing Xcode

To make things progress more smoothly, let's start off by installing Xcode for Mac. Along with Apple's IDE, it will also install the most commonly-used developer tools on the Mac. Make sure you have at least OS X 10.10 (Yosemite), and locate Xcode in the App Store, as shown in the following screenshot:

This will take quite some time to download and install. I'd recommend taking the time to enjoy a nice cup of coffee or working on another project side-by-side.

Installing Xcode installs the iOS SDK, which is a requirement for iOS development in general. As a restriction from Apple, the iOS SDK can only run on a Mac. Xamarin has done everything possible to make sure they follow Apple's guidelines for iOS, such as dynamic code generation. Xamarin's tools also leverage features of Xcode wherever possible to avoid reinventing the wheel.

Installing Xamarin on Mac OS X

After installing Xcode, there are several other dependencies that need to be installed, prior to developing with Xamarin's tooling. Luckily, Xamarin has improved the experience by creating a simple all-in-one installer.

Install Xamarin by performing the following steps:

1. Go to `http://xamarin.com` and click on the large **Download Xamarin** button.
2. Fill out some basic information about yourself and click **Download Xamarin Studio for OS X**.
3. Download `XamarinInstaller.dmg` and mount the disk image.
4. Launch the `Xamarin.app` and accept any OS X security warnings that appear.
5. Progress through the installer; the default options will work fine. You can optionally install `Xamarin.Mac`, but that topic is not covered in this book.

The Xamarin installer will download and install prerequisites such as the Mono runtime, Java, the Android SDK (including the Android emulator and tools), and everything else you need to be up and running.

You will end up with something similar to what is shown in the following screenshot, and we can move on to conquer bigger topics in cross-platform development:

Setting up the Android emulator

The Android emulator has historically been known to be sluggish compared to developing on a physical device. To help solve this issue, Google has produced an x86 emulator that supports hardware acceleration on desktop computers. It isn't installed by default in the **Android Virtual Device** (**AVD**) Manager, so let's set that up.

The x86 Android emulator can be installed by performing the following steps:

1. Open Xamarin Studio.
2. Launch **Tools | Open Android SDK Manager...**.
3. Scroll down to **Extras**; install **Intel x86 Emulator Accelerator (HAXM Installer)**.
4. Scroll to **Android 6.0 (API 23)**; install **Intel x86 Atom System Image**.
5. Optionally, install any other packages you are interested in. At the minimum, make sure you have everything that the Android SDK Manager selects for you to install by default.
6. Close the **Android SDK Manager** and navigate to your Android SDK directory, by default located at `~/Library/Developer/Xamarin/android-sdk-macosx`.
7. Navigate to `extras/intel/Hardware_Accelerated_Execution_Manager` and launch `IntelHAXM_6.0.3.dmg` to install the HAXM driver.
8. Switch back to Xamarin Studio and launch **Tools | Open Google Emulator Manager...**.
9. Click on **Create...**.
10. Enter an AVD name of your choice, such as `x86 Emulator`.
11. Pick a generic device that will be appropriately sized for your display, such as the **Nexus 5**.
12. As **CPU/ABI**, make sure you select an option that supports **Intel Atom (x86)**.
13. After creating the device, go ahead and click on **Start...** to make sure the emulator runs properly.

 These instructions should be very similar on Windows. By default, the Android SDK is installed at `C:\Program Files (x86)\Android\android-sdk` on Windows. Likewise, the HAXM installer is named `intelhaxm-android.exe` on Windows.

The emulator will take some time to start up, so it is a good idea to leave the emulator running while working on an Android project. Xamarin is using the standard Android tools here, so even Java developers feel the pain of the sluggish emulator. If everything starts properly, you will see an Android boot screen followed by a virtual Android device ready for deploying applications from Xamarin Studio, as shown in the following screenshot:

There are many options out there for Android emulators, such as Genymotion or Visual Studio Android Emulator. Using Xamarin will not limit your choices in Android emulators, so feel free to experiment if the default Android emulator isn't working for you.

Installing Xamarin on Windows

Since Microsoft acquired Xamarin in 2016, Xamarin is included with any edition of Visual Studio. The editions are as follows:

- **Visual Studio Community**: This is a free version available to anyone. There are restrictions for using this edition for companies.
- **Visual Studio Professional**: This is the general edition companies should use. On the Visual Studio side, it includes features for Team Foundation Server.
- **Visual Studio Enterprise**: Contains additional features in both Visual Studio and Xamarin. Xamarin features include embedded assemblies, the live Xamarin Inspector, and the Xamarin profiler.

When first setting up a Windows PC for Xamarin development, there are two choices to consider. If you already have Visual Studio, then you can merely use the Xamarin installer to add the necessary Visual Studio extensions and item templates to your existing installation. If you do not have Visual Studio installed yet, then there is simply an option in the Visual Studio 2015 installer for installing Xamarin.

If you want to install from the Visual Studio installer:

1. Download your desired version of Visual Studio from `https://www.visualstud io.com/downloads/`.
2. Run the Visual Studio installer.
3. Under **Cross Platform Mobile Development**, make sure to select **C#/.NET (Xamarin v4.1.0)** (the version number will change according to the version you use). This should automatically select the Android SDK and other components you will need for Xamarin development.
4. You may also choose to install other useful tools such as **Microsoft Web Developer Tools** or **Universal Windows App Development** tools for targeting Windows 10.

Your installer should look something like this before you click **Next**:

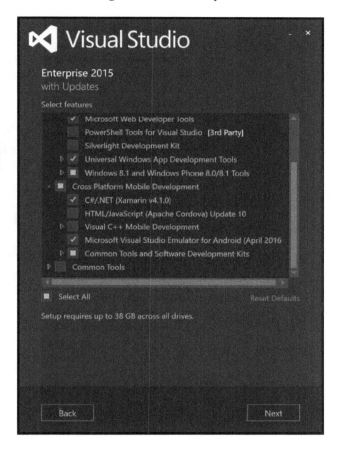

The second option for installing Xamarin is from Xamarin's website:

1. Download the Xamarin installer for Windows from https://xamarin.com/download.
2. Run `XamarinInstaller.exe`, which will download and install all required components on your PC.

The Xamarin installer is a very similar experience to what you see on Mac OS X, and should be very straightforward. It will add Xamarin to an existing Visual Studio installation if needed and install Xamarin Studio.

Connecting Visual Studio to a Mac for iOS development

iOS development requires Xcode running on Mac OS X. Luckily, Xamarin has made remote development possible from a Windows PC.

To connect your PC to a Mac:

1. First open or create a Xamarin.iOS project.
2. Visual Studio will automatically prompt **Xamarin Mac Agent Instructions**.
3. Follow the detailed instructions and screenshots in Visual Studio to enable remote login on your Mac.
4. A **Xamarin Mac Agent** dialog should appear with your Mac's address listed.
5. Click **Connect...** and enter your username and password for your Mac.

When connected, you should see something like the following screenshot:

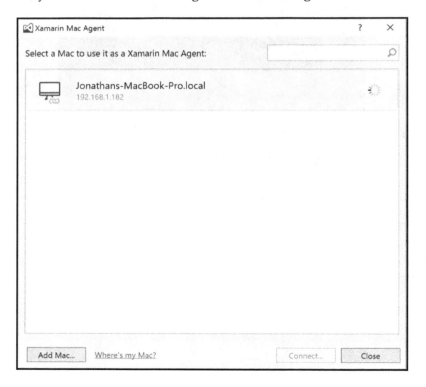

Once connected, you can simply press the play button to debug your project against the iOS simulator or an iOS device of your choice. All the features in Visual Studio you expect will also work with iOS development: break points, mouse-over evaluation, add watch, and so on.

Enrolling in the iOS developer program

To deploy to an iOS device, Apple requires membership to its iOS Developer Program. Membership is $99 USD per year and gives you access to deploy 200 devices for development purposes. You also get access to test servers for implementing more advanced iOS features such as in-app purchases, push notifications, and iOS Game Center. Testing your Xamarin.iOS applications on a physical device is important, so I recommend that you get an account prior to starting iOS development. Performance is very different in a simulator running on your desktop versus a real mobile device. There are also a few Xamarin-specific optimizations that only occur when running on a real device. We'll fully cover the reasons for testing your apps on devices in later chapters.

Since iOS 9, Apple has created a way to sideload apps from iOS devices from any Apple ID. It is recommended only to be used for testing purposes on a few devices, and there is no way to test advanced features such as in-app purchases or push notifications. If you are just toying with iOS, however; it is a good way to get started without paying the $99 developer fee.

Signing up for the iOS developer program can be performed through the following steps:

1. Go to https://developer.apple.com/programs/ios.
2. Click on **Enroll**.
3. Sign in with an existing iTunes account or create a new one. This can't be changed later, so choose the one that is appropriate for your company.
4. Enroll either as an individual or a company. Both are priced at $99, but registering as a company will require paperwork to be faxed to Apple with the assistance of your company's accountant.
5. Review the developer agreement.
6. Fill out Apple's survey for developers.
7. Purchase the $99 developer registration.
8. Wait for a confirmation e-mail.

You should receive an e-mail that looks something like the following screenshot within two business days:

From here, you can continue setting up your account:

1. Either click on **Log in now** from the e-mail you received or go to `https://itunes connect.apple.com`.
2. Log in with your iTunes account.
3. Agree to any additional agreements that appear on the home page of your dashboard.
4. From the iTunes Connect dashboard, go to **Agreements, Tax, and Banking**.
5. In this section, you will see three columns, for **Contact Info**, **Bank Info**, and **Tax Info**.
6. Fill out the appropriate information for your account in all of these sections. Assistance from an accountant will most likely be needed for a company account.

When all is said and done, your **Agreements, Tax, and Banking** section should look something like the following screenshot:

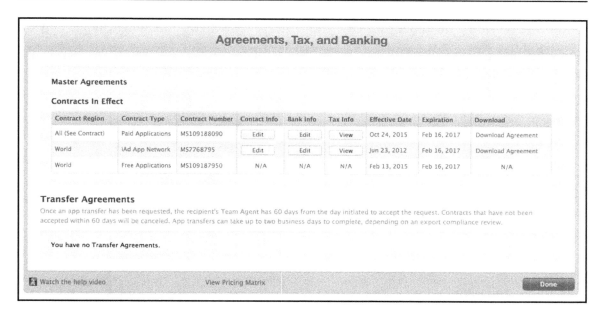

With your iOS developer account successfully registered, you will now be able to deploy to iOS devices and publish your apps to the Apple App Store.

Registering as a Google Play developer

Unlike iOS, deploying your applications to Android devices is free and only requires a few changes in your device settings. A Google Play developer account has only a one-time fee of $25 and doesn't have to be renewed each year. However, just like iOS, you will need a Google Play account to develop in-app purchases, push notifications, or Google Play Game Services. I would recommend setting up an account ahead of time if you inevitably plan on submitting an app to Google Play or need to implement one of these features.

To register as a developer for Google Play, perform the following steps:

1. Go to https://play.google.com/apps/publish.
2. Log in with an existing Google account, or create a new one. This can't be changed later, so choose the one that is appropriate for your company, if needed.
3. Accept the agreement and enter your credit card information.
4. Choose a developer name and enter other important information for your account. Again, choose names appropriate for your company to be seen by users in the app store.

If you get everything filled out correctly, you will end up with the following Google Play Developer Console:

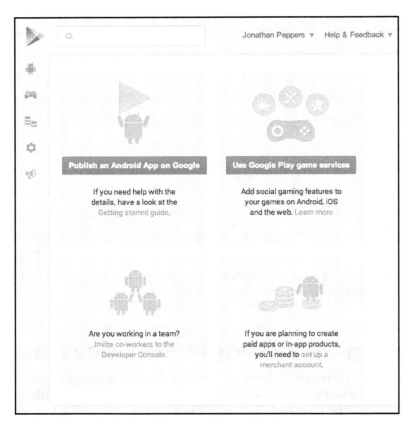

If you plan on selling paid apps or in-app purchases, at this point, I would recommend setting up your **Google Merchant Account**. This will enable Google to pay you the proceeds toward your app sales by applying the appropriate tax laws in your country. If setting this up for your company, I would recommend getting the assistance of your company's accountant or bookkeeper.

The following are the steps to set up a Google Merchant Account:

1. Click on the **set up a merchant account** button.
2. Log in with your Google account a second time.
3. Fill out the appropriate information for selling apps: address, phone number, tax information, and a display name to appear on your customers' credit card bills.

When done, you will notice that the help tip for setting up a merchant account is now missing from the developer console, as shown in the following screenshot:

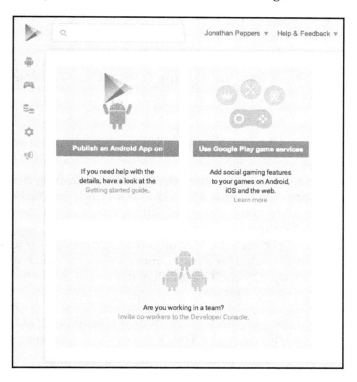

At this point, one would think our account would be fully set up, but there is one more crucial step prior to being able to sell apps: we have to enter the banking information.

Setting up banking for your Google Merchant Account can be performed with the following steps:

1. Go back to the Google Play **Developer Console** at https://play.google.com/apps/publish.
2. Click on the **Financial Reports** section.
3. Click on the small link titled **Visit your merchant account for details**.
4. You should see a warning indicating that you do not have a bank account set up. Click on the **Specify a Bank Account** link to get started.
5. Enter your banking information. Again, a company accountant might be needed.
6. In a few days, look for a small deposit in your account from Google.
7. Confirm the amount by going to http://checkout.google.com/sell.

8. Click on the **Settings** tab, then **Financials**.
9. Next, click on **Verify Account**.
10. Enter the amount that appeared in your bank account and click on **Verify deposit**.

Your Google Merchant Account is also the place where you can cancel or refund customer orders. Google Play is different from the iOS App Store in that all customer issues are directed to the developers.

Summary

In this chapter, we discussed Xamarin's core products for developing Android and iOS applications in C# whether you are using Mac OS X or a Windows PC. We installed Xcode and then ran the Xamarin all-in-one installer, which installs Java, the Android SDK, Xamarin Studio, Xamarin.iOS, and Xamarin.Android. On Windows, we set up Xamarin for use inside Visual Studio and connected a Mac on our local network for iOS development. We set up the x86 Android emulator for a faster, more fluid experience when debugging applications. Finally, we set up iOS and Google Play developer accounts for distributing our applications.

In this chapter, you should have acquired everything you need to get started on building cross-platform applications with Xamarin. Your development computer should be ready to go and you should have all the native SDKs installed and ready for creating the next great app to take the world by storm.

The concepts in this chapter will set us up for more advanced topics, which will require the proper software installed as well as developer accounts with Apple and Google. We will be deploying applications to real devices and implementing more advanced features such as push notifications. In the following chapter, we'll create our first iOS and Android application and cover the basics of each platform.

2
Hello, Platforms!

If you are familiar with developing applications using Visual Studio on Windows, then using Xamarin Studio should be very straightforward. Xamarin uses the same concept of a **solution** containing one or more **projects**, and it has created several new project types for iOS and Android applications. There are also several project templates to jump-start your development of common applications.

Xamarin Studio supports several out-of-the-box project types, including standard .NET class libraries and console applications. You cannot natively develop Windows applications on a Mac with Xamarin Studio, but you can certainly develop the shared code portion of your application in Xamarin Studio. We'll focus on sharing code in the later chapters, but keep in mind that Xamarin enables you to share a common C# backend between most platforms that support C#.

In this chapter, we will cover:

- Creating a simple calculator application for iOS
- Apple's MVC pattern
- Xcode and storyboards
- Creating a calculator application for Android
- Android activities
- Xamarin's Android designer

Building your first iOS application

Launch Xamarin Studio and start a new solution. Just like in Visual Studio, there are lots of project types that can be created from the **New Solution** dialog. Xamarin Studio, formerly **MonoDevelop**, supports the development of many different types of projects such as C# applications targeting the Mono runtime or .NET Core, NUnit test projects, and even other languages besides C#, such as VB or C++.

Xamarin Studio supports the following project types for iOS:

- **Single View App**: This is the basic project type that sets up an iOS storyboard along with a single view and controller.
- **Master Detail App**: a project type containing a list of items that you can tap to view details about. On iPhone/iPod it will use multiple controls taking up the full screen area and the iOS `UISplitViewController` on iPad.
- **Tabbed App**: This is a project type that automatically sets up a `UITabViewController` for applications with a tab layout.
- **Page-Based App**: This project type automatically sets up a `UIPageViewController` for paging between screens as a carousel.
- **WebView App**: This project type is for creating "hybrid" applications that are partially HTML and partially native. The application is set up to take advantage of the Razor templating features of Xamarin Studio.
- **Class Library**: This is a class library used within other iOS application projects.
- **Bindings Library**: This is an iOS project that can create C# bindings for an Objective-C library.
- **UI Test App**: An NUnit test project for running UI tests either locally or on Xamarin Test Cloud.
- **Unit Test App**: This is a special iOS application project that can run NUnit tests.

To get started, create a new solution and navigate to **iOS** | **App**, and create a **Single View App** as seen in the following screenshot:

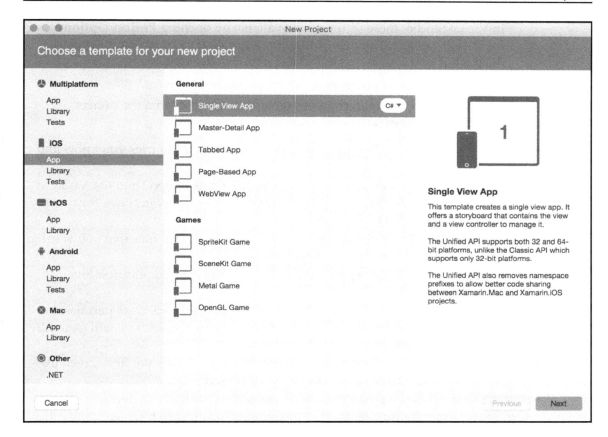

In Visual Studio, you can create the correct type of project from **Visual C#** **I iOS I Universal I Single View App** in the new solution dialog.

In the next step, we will need to:

1. Choose an **App Name**.
2. Choose an **Organizational Identifier**, which is a "reverse" domain name to uniquely identify your app.
3. Select which iOS devices you want to support; you can keep the default.
4. Select the minimum iOS version you want to support; you can keep the default.
5. Finally, on the last step, choose a directory to put your project and click **Create**.

In Visual Studio, these settings are available by opening **Project Options** for the iOS project. Xamarin Studio has additional steps in its new project dialog, but you can always edit these settings after the fact.

You'll notice that several files and folders are automatically created from the project template. These files are as follows:

- `References`: These are the standard references to other libraries you know and love from .NET.
- `Components`: This folder will contain any components added from the Xamarin Component store. See `Chapter 9`, *Web Services with Push Notifications*, for more info about the Xamarin Component store.
- `Resources`: This directory will contain any images or plain files that you want to be copied directly to your application bundle.
- `AppDelegate.cs`: This is Apple's main class for handling application-level events in your app.
- `Entitlements.plist`: This is a settings file Apple uses to declare permissions for certain iOS features such as push notifications and iCloud. You will generally only have to use it for advanced iOS features.
- `*ViewController.cs`: This is the controller that represents the first screen in your app. It will have the same name as your project.
- `Info.plist`: This is Apple's version of a **manifest** file that can declare various settings for your application such as the app title, icon, splash screens, and other common settings.
- `LaunchScreen.storyboard`: This is a storyboard file for laying out the splash screen for your application. By default, Xamarin's project template puts the name of your project here.
- `Main.cs`: This file contains the standard entry point for a C# program: `static void Main()`. It's most likely that you will not need to modify this file.
- `MainStoryboard.storyboard`: This is the storyboard definition file for your application. It will contain the layouts for the views in your app, list of controllers, and the transitions for navigating throughout your app. A storyboard is exactly how it sounds: a diagram/flowchart of the different screens in your iOS application.

Now, let's run the application to see what we get by default from the project template. Click on the large play button in the top-left corner of Xamarin Studio. You will be greeted by the simulator running your first iOS application as seen in the following screenshot:

So far, your app is just a plain white screen, which is not very exciting or useful. Let's get a little more background on iOS development before moving forward.

Depending on your application's minimum iOS target, you can also run the application on different versions of the iOS simulator. Apple also provides simulators for iPad and all the different iOS devices currently in the market. It is also important to know that these are simulators and not emulators. An emulator will run an encapsulated version of the mobile OS (just as Android does). Emulators generally exhibit slower performance but give you a closer replica of the real OS. Apple's simulators run as native Mac applications and are not true operating systems. The benefit is that they are very fast in comparison to Android emulators.

Understanding Apple's MVC pattern

Before getting too far with iOS development, it is really important to get a foundation on Apple's design pattern for developing on iOS. You might have used the **Model View Controller (MVC)** pattern with other technologies such as **ASP.NET**, but Apple implements this paradigm in a slightly different way. Apples core set of APIs for developing UIs for iOS applications is called UIKit. Xamarin applications can take full advantage of UIKit by directly using these APIs from C#. UIKit is heavily based on the MVC design pattern.

The **MVC** design pattern includes the following:

- **Model**: This is the backend business logic driving the application. This can be any code that, for example, makes web requests to a server or saves data to a local **SQLite** database.
- **View**: This is the actual user interface seen on the screen. In iOS terms, this is any class that derives from `UIView`. Examples are toolbars, buttons, and anything else the user would see on the screen and interact with.
- **Controller**: This is the workhorse of the **MVC** pattern. The controller interacts with the **Model** layer and updates the **View** layer with the results. Similar to the **View** layer, any controller class would derive from `UIViewController`. This is where a good portion of the code in iOS applications resides.

The following image shows the MVC design pattern:

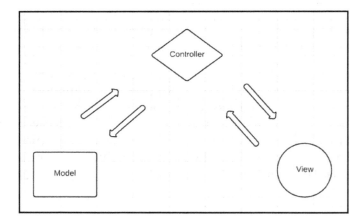

To understand this pattern better, let's walk through the following example of a common scenario:

1. We have an iOS application with a search box that needs to query a website for a list of jobs.
2. The user will enter some text into the `UITextField` textbox and click on the `UIButton` button to start the search. This is the **View** layer.
3. Some code will respond to the button by interacting with the **View**, display a `UIActivityIndicatorView` spinner, and call a method in another class to perform the search. This is the **Controller** layer.
4. A web request will be made in the called class and a list of jobs will be returned asynchronously. This is the **Model** layer.
5. The **Controller** will then update the **View** with the list of jobs and hide the spinner.

 For more information on Apple's MVC pattern, see the documentation site at `https://developer.apple.com/library/mac/documentation/genera l/conceptual/devpedia-cocoacore/MVC.html`.

A point to note is that you are free to do anything you want in the model layer of your application. This is where we can use plain C# classes that can be reused on other platforms such as Android. This includes any functionality using the C# **Base Class Libraries** (**BCL**), such as working with web services or a database. We'll dive deeper into cross-platform architecture and code-sharing concepts later in the book.

Using the iOS designer

Since our plain white application is quite boring, let's modify the view layer of our application with some controls. To do this, we will modify the `MainStoryboard.storyboard` file in your project in Xamarin Studio or Visual Studio. Optionally, you can open the storyboard file in Xcode, which was previously the method of editing storyboard files before the Xamarin.iOS designer. Using Xcode could still be useful if there is a feature in iOS storyboards which isn't available in the Xamarin designer, or if you need to edit an older iOS format such as XIB files. However, Xcode is not quite as good of an experience, since custom controls in Xcode render as plain, white squares. Xamarin's designer actually runs your drawing code in custom controls, so that you get an accurate view of what your application will look like at runtime.

Let's add some controls to our app by performing the following steps:

1. Open the project you created earlier in this chapter in Xamarin Studio.
2. Double-click on the `MainStoryboard.storyboard` file.
3. The iOS designer will open, and you will see the layout for the single controller in your application.
4. In the **Document Outline** tab on the right, you'll see that your controller contains a single view in its layout hierarchy.
5. In the top-left corner, you'll notice a toolbox containing several types of objects that you can drag-and-drop onto your controller's view.
6. In the search box, search for `UILabel` and drag the label centered at the top of the screen.
7. Double-click on the label to edit the text of the label to the number zero (**0**). You can also fill out this value from the **Properties** tab in the bottom right.
8. Likewise, search for `UIButton` and create 10 buttons numbered **0-9** to create a number pad. You may edit the text on the button by using the **Properties** tab. You can also use **Copy/Paste** to speed up creating them. Double-clicking the button would add a click event handler, which you might be familiar with from Visual Studio when developing for other platforms.
9. Run the application.

Your application should start looking a lot more like a real application (a calculator) as seen in the following screenshot:

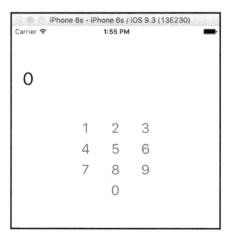

In Visual Studio on Windows, these steps are identical to Xamarin Studio on a Mac. Keep in mind that you must remain connected to a Mac on your local network to use the Xamarin.iOS designer. Instructions for connecting to a Mac are in `Chapter 1`, *Xamarin Setup*.

Now you might be wondering about adding user interaction options to the app at this point. In Xcode's iOS designer, you would make an **outlet** that makes each view visible from C#. An outlet is a reference to a view in a storyboard or XIB file that will be filled out with an instance of the view at runtime. You can compare this concept to naming a control in other technologies such as **ASP.NET**, **WebForms**, or **WPF** (**Windows Presentation Foundation**). Luckily Xamarin's iOS designer is a bit simpler than setting up an outlet in Xcode. You merely fill out the **Name** field in the **Properties** tab, and Xamarin Studio will generate a property in a **partial class**, which gives you access to the label and button from your controller. Additionally, you can wire an **action** from a storyboard file, which is a method that will be called when an event occurs. Xamarin Studio exposes iOS actions as partial methods to be implemented in your classes.

Let's add some interactions to the app as follows:

1. Switch back to Xamarin Studio.
2. Double-click on the `MainStoryboard.storyboard` file again.
3. Select the label you created earlier and navigate to the **Properties** pane and make sure you have the **Widget** tab selected.
4. Enter the name `label` in the **Name** field.
5. Create a new button with the text **+** for addition.
6. Change to the **Events** tab.
7. Enter the name `OnAdd` into its **Up Inside** field. You can remember this as the "click" event for the button.
8. Xamarin Studio will direct you on where to place the `OnAdd` method in your `UIViewController`.
9. Repeat this process for each of the number buttons, but name the **Up Inside** event `OnNumber`.
10. Create a new button with the text **=** for the calculator.
11. Change to the **Events** tab.
12. Enter the name `OnEquals` into its **Up Inside** field.

Xamarin has improved this experience greatly from what the experience used to be in Xcode. Xcode has a strange interface for those more familiar with tools like Visual Studio. The method for creating an outlet involved clicking and dragging from the control onto an Objective-C header file. Merely filling out a **Name** field is much simpler and much more intuitive for developers that have a C# background.

Now that we have two outlets defined, two new properties will be available from your controller. Expand the *ViewController.cs file in your solution and open the *ViewController.designer.cs file. You will see your properties defined as follows:

```
[Outlet]
[GeneratedCode ("iOS Designer", "1.0")]
MonoTouch.UIKit.UILabel label { get; set; }
```

It is not a good idea to modify this file since the IDE will rebuild it if you make further changes in the designer or Xcode. Nevertheless, it is good practice to learn how things are actually working behind the scenes.

Open your *ViewController.cs file, and let's enter the following code in your controller's method:

```
partial void OnAdd(UIButton sender)
{
    if (!string.IsNullOrEmpty(label.Text))
    {
        label.Text += "+";
    }
}

partial void OnNumber(UIButton sender)
{
    if (string.IsNullOrEmpty(label.Text) || label.Text == "0")
    {
        label.Text = sender.CurrentTitle;
    }
    else
    {
        label.Text += sender.CurrentTitle;
    }
}

partial void OnEquals(UIButton sender)
{
    //Simple logic for adding up the numbers
    string[] split = label.Text.Split('+');
    int sum = 0;
    foreach (string text in split)
```

```
    {
        int x;
        if (int.TryParse(text, out x))
            sum += x;
    }
    label.Text = sum.ToString();
}
```

Most of this code is just general C# logic for making a calculator operate. In the `OnAdd` method we append a + symbol if the label's text is non-empty. In the `OnNumber` method we replace or append to the label's text appropriately. Finally, in the `OnEquals` method we calculate the expression residing in the label with a string split operation and integer conversion. We then place the result in the label's text.

Run your application, and you will be able to interact with your calculator as shown in the following screenshot:

Now would be a good time to complete this exercise on your own and finish the calculator. Adding buttons for subtraction, multiplication, division, and a "clear" button would complete the simple calculator. This should get you a handle on working with Apple's APIs for `UIButton`, `UILabel`, and basics of the UIKit framework.

Since we have gone over the basics of laying out controls in Xamarin's iOS designer and interacting with outlets in C#, let's go over the standard life cycle of an iOS application. The primary location for handling application-level events is in the `AppDelegate` class.

If you open your `AppDelegate.cs` file, you can override the following methods:

- `FinishedLaunching`: This is the first entry point for the application, which should return `true`.
- `DidEnterBackground`: This means the user clicked on the home button on their device or another app, such as a phone call, came to the foreground. You should perform any action needed to save the user's progress or state of the UI as the iOS may kill your application once pushed to the background. While your application is in the background, the user could be navigating through the home screen or opening other apps. Your application is effectively paused in memory until resumed by the user.
- `WillEnterForeground`: This means the user has reopened your application from the background. You might need to perform other actions here such as refreshing the data on the screen and so on.
- `OnResignActivation`: This happens if the operating system displays a system popup on top of your application. Examples of this are calendar reminders or the menu the user can swipe down from the top of the screen.
- `OnActivated`: This happens immediately after the `OnResignActivation` method is executed as the user returns to your app.
- `ReceiveMemoryWarning`: This is a warning from the operating system to free up the memory in your application. It is not commonly needed with Xamarin because of the C#'s garbage collector, but if there are any heavy objects such as images throughout your app, this is a good place to dispose them. If enough memory cannot be freed, the operating system could terminate your application.
- `HandleOpenUrl`: This is called if you implement a **URL scheme**, which is the iOS equivalent of file extension associations on a desktop platform. If you register your app for opening different types of files or URLs, this method will be called.

Likewise, in your `*ViewController.cs` file, you can override the following methods on your controller:

- `ViewDidLoad`: This occurs when the view associated with your controller is loaded. It will occur only once on devices running iOS 6 or higher.
- `ViewWillAppear`: This occurs prior to your view appearing on the screen. If there are any views that need to be refreshed while navigating throughout your app, this is generally the best place to do it.
- `ViewDidAppear`: This occurs after the completion of any transition animations and your view is displayed on the screen. In some uncommon situations, you might need to perform actions here instead of in `ViewWillAppear`.

- `ViewWillDisappear`: This method is called prior to your view being hidden. You might need to perform some clean-up operations here.
- `ViewDidDisappear`: This occurs after any transition animations are completed for displaying a different controller on the screen. Just like the methods for appearing, this occurs after `ViewWillDisappear`.

There are several more methods available to override, but many are deprecated for newer versions of iOS. Familiarize yourself with Apple's documentation site at http://developer.apple.com/library/ios. It is very helpful to read the documentation on each class and method when trying to understand how Apple's APIs work. Learning how to read (not necessarily code) Objective-C is also a useful skill to learn so that you are able to convert Objective-C examples to C# when developing iOS applications.

Building your first Android application

Setting up an Android application in Xamarin Studio is just as easy as it is for iOS and is very similar to the experience in Visual Studio. Xamarin Studio includes several project templates that are specific for Android to jump-start your development.

Xamarin Studio includes the following project templates:

- **Android App**: A standard Android application that targets the newest Android SDKs installed on your machine.
- **Wear App**: A project targeting Android Wear, for smartwatch devices.
- **WebView App**: A project template for a hybrid app using HTML for certain parts. Support for Razor templating is available.
- **Class Library**: A class library that can only be referenced by Android application projects.
- **Bindings Library**: A project for setting up a Java library to be called from C#.
- **UI Test App**: an NUnit test project for running UI tests either locally or on Xamarin Test Cloud.
- **Unit Test App**: This is a special Android application project that can run NUnit tests.

Launch Xamarin Studio and start a new solution. From the **New Solution** dialog, create a new **Android App** under the **Android** section. Select

You will end up with a solution looking something like the following screenshot:

In Visual Studio, the Android project template is found under **Android |
Blank App**.

You'll notice that the following files and folders specific to Android have been created for
you:

- The `Components` folder. This is the same as for iOS projects, the place for adding
  components from the Xamarin Component Store.
- The `Assets` folder: This directory will contain files with a `build` action of
  `AndroidAsset`. This folder will contain raw files to be bundled with an Android
  application.
- `Properties/AndroidManifest.xml`: This file contains standard declarations
  about your Android applications, such as the application name, ID, and
  permissions.
- The `Resources` folder: Resources are images, layouts, strings, and so on that can
  be loaded via Android's resource system. Each file will have an ID generated in
  `Resources.designer.cs` that you can use to load the resource.
- The `Resources/drawable` folder: Any images used by your application are
  generally placed here.

- The `Resources/layout` folder: This contains any `*.axml` (Android XML) files that Android uses for declaring UIs. Layouts can be for an entire **activity**, **fragment, dialog,** or **child control** to be displayed on the screen.
- `Resources/mipmap-*` folders: Contain icons for your application to be displayed on different Android devices' home screens. App icons in these because they are used at resolutions different from the device's current density.
- The `Resources/values` folder: This contains XML files to declare key-value pairs for strings (and other types) throughout an application. This is how localization for multiple languages is normally set up on Android.
- `MainActivity.cs`: This is the `MainLauncher` action and the first activityof your Android application. There is no `static void Main` function in Android apps; execution begins on the activity that has `MainLauncher` set to `true`.

Now let's perform the following steps to run the application:

1. Click on the play button to compile and run the application.
2. A **Select Device** dialog may appear.
3. Select the emulator of your choice and click on **Start Emulator**. If you have set up the x86 emulator in `Chapter 1`, *Xamarin Setup*, I would recommend using it.
4. Wait a few seconds for the emulator to start. Once it starts, it is a good idea to leave it running as long as you are working on an Android project. This will save you a good deal of time waiting.
5. You should see the emulator now enabled in the list of devices; select it, and click on **OK**.
6. The very first time you deploy to an emulator or device, Xamarin Studio will have to install a few things such as the Mono shared runtime and Android platform tools.
7. Switch over to the Android emulator.
8. Your application will appear.

In Visual Studio on Windows, you might also try using the **Visual Studio Emulator for Android**. It is a nice emulator that comes preinstalled with Visual Studio 2015.

When all is done, you have deployed your first Android application, complete with a single button. Your app will look like the following screenshot:

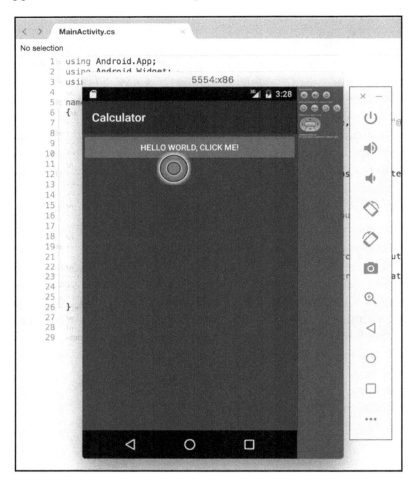

Understanding Android activities

The Android operating system is very focused on the concept of an activity. An activity is a task or unit of work that users can perform on their screen. For example, users would perform a **phone activity** for dialing a number and carry out a second activity for interacting with their address book to locate the number. Each Android application is a collection of one or more activities that users can launch and press the hardware's back key on their device to exit or cancel. The user's history is kept in the Android **back stack**, which you can manipulate from code in special cases. When a new activity starts, the previous one is paused and maintained in memory for later use, unless the operating system is running low on memory.

Activities are loosely coupled with each other; in some ways, you can think of them as having completely separate states from one another in memory. Static classes, properties, and fields will persist the life of the application, but the common practice is to pass a state in an Android **bundle**. This is useful for passing an identifier for an item displayed in a list to edit that item in a new activity.

Activities have the following lifecycle callback methods that you can override:

- `OnCreate`: This is the first method called when your activity is created. Set up your views and perform other loading logic here. Most importantly, you will call `SetContentView` here to set up your activity's view.
- `OnResume`: This is called when your activity's view is visible on the screen. It is called if your activity is displayed for the first time, and when the user returns to it from another activity.
- `OnPause`: This is called to notify that the user has left your activity. It can happen prior to navigating to a new activity within your app, locking the screen, or hitting the home button. Assume that the user may not return, so you need to save any changes the user made here.
- `OnStart`: This occurs immediately before `OnResume` when the activity's view is about to be displayed on the screen. It occurs when an activity starts and when a user returns to it from another activity.
- `OnStop`: This occurs immediately after `OnPause` when the activity's view is no longer displayed on the screen.
- `OnRestart`: This method occurs when the user returns to your activity from a previous activity.
- `OnActivityResult`: This method is used for communicating with other activities in other applications on Android. It is used in conjunction with `StartActvityForResult`; for example, you would use this to interact with the Facebook application to log in a user.
- `OnDestroy`: This is called when your activity is about to be freed from memory. Perform any additional clean-up that could help the operating system here, such as disposing of any other heavyweight objects the activity was using.

A flowchart of the Android lifecycle is as follows:

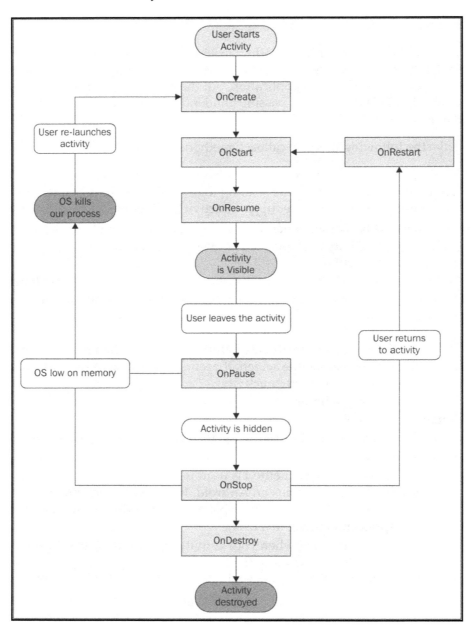

Unlike iOS, Android does not enforce any design patterns upon its developers. However, it is not possible to make it by without understanding the Android activity lifecycle to some degree. Many concepts with activities have a parallel to controllers on iOS; for example, `OnStart` is equivalent to `ViwWillAppear` and `OnResume` is equivalent to `ViewDidAppear`.

Other methods of note for working with activities are as follows:

- `StartActivity(Type type)`: This method starts a new activity within your application and passes no extra information to the activity.
- `StartActivity(Intent intent)`: This is an overload method for starting a new activity with `Intent`. This gives you the ability to pass additional information to the new activity, and you can also launch activities in other applications.
- `StartActivityForResult`: This method starts a new activity with the anticipation of receiving `OnActivityResult` when the activity's operation is completed.
- `Finish`: This will close the current activity and invoke `OnDestroy` when it is completely closed and no longer displayed on the screen. Depending on what is currently on the back stack, the user will return to a previous activity or the home screen.
- `SetContentView`: This method sets the primary view to be displayed for an activity. It should be called within the `OnCreate` method prior to the activity being displayed on the screen.
- `FindViewById`: This is a method for locating the view displayed in your activity. It has a generic version for returning a view of the appropriate type.

You can think of `intent` as an object that describes the transition from one activity to another. You can pass additional data through intents as well as modify how the activity is displayed and the user's navigation history.

In addition to activities, Android has the concept of a fragment. You can think of a fragment to be a miniature activity that is displayed inside a parent activity. Fragments are useful for reusing different pieces of a UI throughout your apps and can also help you implement split screen navigation on tablets.

Xamarin's Android designer

The default template for Android projects has a little more built-in functionality than iOS, so we will have a few controls to remove later. Android user interface layouts are defined in XML files that are readable by humans and editable. However, Xamarin Studio has provided an excellent design tool that allows you to drag-and-drop controls to define your Android layouts. Let's add some more features to your application and start using the Android designer.

Return to Xamarin Studio and carry out the following steps to add features to your app:

1. Open the Android project you created earlier in this chapter in Xamarin Studio.
2. Under **Resources | layout** in your project, open `Main.axml`.
3. You will see the Android designer open in Xamarin Studio.
4. Delete the existing label and button from the Android project template.
5. Drag **TextView** from the **Toolbox** section on the right to the empty layout.
6. Type some default text such as `0` into the label.
7. In the **Properties** pane on the right, you'll see the **id** value is set to `@+id/textView1`. Let's change it to `@+id/text` so we can later interact with the label in C#.
8. Now drag a **GridLayout** from the **Toolbox** section and under the **Properties** panel set **Row Count** to 4 and **Column** to 3.
9. Drag 10 **Button** widgets from the **Toolbox** section and number their text **0-9**.
10. Set their **id** to `@+id/button0` numbered from **0-9**.
11. Create two more buttons with ids `@+id/plus` and `@+id/equals`, with their text set to **+** and **=** respectively.

> In Visual Studio, the Xamarin.Android designer is mostly identical to its Xamarin Studio counterpart. The main difference is when editing the properties on a control, the standard Visual Studio properties editor is used. You may find it useful to toggle between **A to Z** and grouped sorting via the toolbar buttons in the **Properties** pane.

Now if you try to compile and run your application, you will notice some compiler errors. For now, open `MainActivity.cs` and remove the code in the `OnCreate` method with the exception of the line calling `SetContentView`.

Your `MainActivity` should look like this:

```
[Activity(Label = "Calculator", MainLauncher = true, Icon =
"@mipmap/icon")]
public class MainActivity : Activity
{
  protected override void OnCreate(Bundle savedInstanceState)
  {
    base.OnCreate(savedInstanceState);
    SetContentView(Resource.Layout.Main);
  }
}
```

Now launch your Android application and it should look identical to the changes you made in the designer as follows:

Switch back to Xamarin Studio and open `MainActivity.cs`. Let's modify the activity to interact with the layouts we set up in the Xamarin.Android designer. We use the `FindViewById` method to retrieve a view by the ID we set up in the layout file. Xamarin Studio has also auto-generated a static class named `Resource` for referencing your identifiers.

First declare a class-level private field in `MainActivity.cs`:

```
TextView text;
```

So let's retrieve the instance of the **TextView** field by placing this code in `OnCreate` as follows:

```
text = FindViewById<TextView>(Resource.Id.text);
```

The `Resource` class is a static class that the Xamarin designer will populate for you. For future reference, you may have to build your Android project for new IDs and other resources to show up in your C# files in Xamarin Studio.

Create a method we'll use for click events, somewhere in `MainActivity.cs`, it will look very similar to what we did on iOS:

```
private void OnNumber(object sender, EventArgs e)
{
    var button = (Button)sender;
    if (string.IsNullOrEmpty(text.Text) || text.Text == "0")
    {
        text.Text = button.Text;
    }
    else
    {
        text.Text += button.Text;
    }
}
```

Next, let's wire up the `Click` event for `number1` in your activity's `OnCreate` method:

```
var button = FindViewById<Button>(Resource.Id.number1);
button.Click += OnNumber;
```

Repeat this code for all number buttons **0-9**.

Next, let's set up event handlers for the "add" and "equals" buttons as we did in the iOS app:

```
private void OnAdd(object sender, EventArgs e)
{
    if (!string.IsNullOrEmpty(text.Text))
    {
        text.Text += "+";
    }
}
```

```
private void OnEquals(object sender, EventArgs e)
{
    //This is the same simple calculator logic as on iOS
    string[] split = text.Text.Split('+');
    int sum = 0;
    foreach (string text in split)
    {
        int x;
        if (int.TryParse(text, out x))
            sum += x;
    }
    text.Text = sum.ToString();
}
```

Next, let's wire up the `Click` event for these buttons in your activity's `OnCreate` method:

```
var add = FindViewById<Button>(Resource.Id.add);
add.Click += OnAdd;
var equals = FindViewById<Button>(Resource.Id.equals);
equals.Click += OnEquals;;
```

Now if we run the application, we'll get an Android app that functions identically to the iOS calculator shown previously in this chapter:

Summary

In this chapter, we created our first iOS application in Xamarin Studio. We covered Apple's MVC design pattern to better understand the relationship between `UIViewController` and `UIView` and also covered how to use the iOS designer in Xamarin Studio for editing storyboard files. Next, we created our first Android application in Xamarin Studio and learned the activity lifecycle in Android. We also used Xamarin's Android designer to make changes to Android XML layouts.

From the topics covered in this chapter, you should be fairly confident in developing simple apps for iOS and Android using Xamarin's tools. You should have a basic understanding of the native SDKs and design patterns to accomplish tasks on iOS and Android.

In the next chapter, we'll cover various techniques for sharing code across platforms with Xamarin Studio. We'll go over different ways for architecting your cross-platform application and how to set up projects and solutions for use in either Visual Studio or Xamarin Studio.

3
Code Sharing Between iOS and Android

Xamarin's tools promise to share a good portion of your code between iOS and Android while taking advantage of the native APIs on each platform where possible. Doing so is an exercise in software engineering more than a programming skill or having the knowledge of each platform. To architect a Xamarin application for enabling code sharing, it is a must to separate your application into distinct layers. We'll cover the basics as well as specific options to consider certain situations.

In this chapter, we will cover:

- The MVVM design pattern for code sharing
- Project and solution organization strategies
- Portable Class Libraries (PCLs)
- Preprocessor statements for platform-specific code
- Dependency Injection (DI) simplified
- Inversion of Control (IoC)

Learning the MVVM design pattern

The **Model-View-ViewModel (MVVM)** design pattern was originally invented for **WPF (Windows Presentation Foundation)** applications using **XAML** for separating the UI from business logic and taking full advantage of **data binding**. Applications architected in this way have a distinct ViewModel layer that has no dependencies on its user interface. This architecture in itself is optimized for unit testing as well as cross-platform development. Since an application's ViewModel classes have no dependencies on the UI layer, you can easily swap an iOS user interface for an Android one and write tests against the ViewModel layer. The MVVM design pattern is also very similar to the MVC design pattern discussed in the previous chapters.

The MVVM design pattern includes the following:

- **Model**: The model layer is the backend business logic driving the application and any business objects to go along with it. This can be anything from making web requests to a server to using a backend database.
- **View**: This layer is the actual user interface seen on the screen. In case of cross-platform development, it includes any platform-specific code for driving the user interface of the application. On iOS, this includes controllers used throughout an application and on Android, an application's activities.
- **ViewModel**: This layer acts as the glue in MVVM applications. The ViewModel layers coordinate operations between the View and Model layers. A ViewModel layer will contain properties that the view will get or set, and functions for each operation that can be made by the user on each view. The ViewModel will also invoke operations on the Model layer if needed.

The following diagram shows the MVVM design pattern:

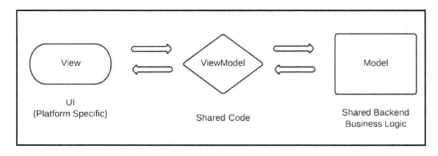

It is important to note that the interaction between the View and ViewModel layers is traditionally created by data binding with WPF. However, iOS and Android do not have built-in data binding mechanisms, so our general approach throughout this book will be to manually call the ViewModel layer from the view. There are a few frameworks out there that provide data binding functionality such as **MVVMCross** and **Xamarin.Forms**.

To understand this pattern better, let's implement a common scenario. Let's say we have a search box on the screen and a search button. When the user enters some text and clicks on the button, a list of products and prices will be displayed to the user. In our example, we will use the **async** and **await** keywords that are available in C# 5 to simplify asynchronous programming.

To implement this feature, we would start with a simple `model` class (also called a `business` object) as follows:

```
public class Product
{
    public int Id { get; set; } //Just a numeric identifier
    public string Name { get; set; } //Name of the product
    public float Price { get; set; } //Price of the product
}
```

Next, we would implement our Model layer for retrieving products based on the search term. This is where the business logic is performed, expressing how the search needs to actually work. This is seen in the following lines of code:

```
// An example class, in the real world would talk to a web
// server or database.
public class ProductRepository
{
  // a sample list of products to simulate a database
  private Product[] products = new[]
  {
    new Product { Id = 1, Name = "Shoes", Price = 19.99f },
    new Product { Id = 2, Name = "Shirt", Price = 15.99f },
    new Product { Id = 3, Name = "Hat", Price = 9.99f },
  };

  public async Task<Product[]> SearchProducts(string searchTerm)
  {
    // Wait 2 seconds to simulate web request
    await Task.Delay(2000);

    // Use Linq-to-objects to search, ignoring case
    searchTerm = searchTerm.ToLower();
```

```
        return products.Where(p =>
            p.Name.ToLower().Contains(searchTerm))
            .ToArray();
    }
}
```

It is important to note here that the `Product` and `ProductRepository` class are both considered as part of the Model layer of a cross-platform application. Some may consider `ProductRepository` as a **service** that is generally a self-contained class for retrieving data. It is a good idea to separate this functionality into two classes. The `Product` class's job is to hold information about a product, while `ProductRepository` is in charge of retrieving products. This is the basis for the **single responsibility principle**, which states that each class should only have one job or concern.

Next, we would implement a `ViewModel` class as follows:

```
public class ProductViewModel
{
    private readonly ProductRepository repository =
        new ProductRepository();

    public string SearchTerm
    {
        get;
        set;
    }

    public Product[] Products
    {
        get;
        private set;
    }

    public async Task Search()
    {
        if (string.IsNullOrEmpty(SearchTerm))
            Products = null;
        else
            Products = await repository.SearchProducts(SearchTerm);
    }
}
```

From here, your platform-specific code starts. Each platform would handle managing an instance of a `ViewModel` class, setting the `SearchTerm` property, and calling `Search` when the button is clicked. When the task completes, the user interface layer would update a list displayed on the screen.

If you are familiar with the MVVM design pattern used with WPF, you might notice that we are not implementing INotifyPropertyChanged for data binding. Since iOS and Android don't have the concept of data binding, we omitted this functionality. If you plan on having a WPF or Windows UWP version of your mobile application or are using a framework that provides data binding, you should implement support for it where needed.

> To learn more about INotifyPropertyChanged, check out this article on MSDN: https://msdn.microsoft.com/en-us/library/system.compone ntmodel.inotifypropertychanged

Comparing project organization strategies

You might be asking yourself at this point, how do I set up my solution in Xamarin Studio to handle shared code and also have platform-specific projects? Xamarin.iOS applications can only reference Xamarin.iOS class libraries; so, setting up a solution can be problematic. There are several strategies for setting up a cross-platform solution, each with its own advantages and disadvantages.

Options for cross-platform solutions are as follows:

- **File Linking**: For this option, you would start with either a plain .NET 4.0 or .NET 4.5 class library containing all the shared code. You would then have a new project for each platform you want your app to run on. Each platform-specific project would have a subdirectory with all of the files linked in from the first class library. To set this up, add the existing files to the project, and select the **Add a link to the file** option. Any unit tests can run against the original class library. The advantages and disadvantages of file linking are as follows:
  - **Advantages**: This approach is very flexible. You can choose to link or not link certain files and can also use preprocessor directives such as #if IPHONE. You can also reference different libraries on Android versus iOS.
  - **Disadvantages**: You have to manage a file's existence in three projects: core library, iOS, and Android. This can be a hassle if it is a large application or if many people are working on it. This option is also a bit outdated since the arrival of shared projects.

- **Cloned Project Files**: It is very similar to file linking, the main difference being that you have a class library for each platform in addition to the main project. By placing the iOS and Android projects in the same directory as the main project, the files can be added without linking. You can easily add files by right-clicking on the solution and selecting **Display Options** | **Show All Files**. Unit tests can run against the original class library or the platform-specific versions:
    - **Advantages**: This approach is just as flexible as file linking, but you don't have to manually link any files. You can still use preprocessor directives and reference different libraries on each platform.
    - **Disadvantages**: You still have to manage a file's existence in three projects. There is additionally some manual file arranging required to set this up. You also end up with an extra project to manage on each platform. This option is also a bit outdated since the arrival of shared projects.
- **Shared Project**: Beginning in Visual Studio 2013, Microsoft created the concept of shared projects to enable code sharing between Windows 8 and Windows Phone apps. Xamarin has also implemented shared projects in Xamarin Studio as another option for enabling code sharing. Shared projects are virtually the same as file linking, in that adding a reference to a shared project effectively adds its files to your project:
    - **Advantages**: This approach is the same as file linking, but a lot cleaner since your shared code is in a single project. Xamarin Studio also provides a dropdown to toggle between each referencing project, so you can see the effect of preprocessor statements in your code.
    - **Disadvantages**: Since all files in a shared project get added to each platform's main project, it can get ugly to include platform specific code in a shared project. Preprocessor statements can quickly get out of hand if you have a large team, or have team members that don't have a lot of experience. A shared project also doesn't compile to a DLL, so there is not a way to distribute this kind of project without the source code.

- **Portable Class Libraries**: This is the most optimal option once you are more experienced with Xamarin; you begin the solution by making a **portable** class library (**PCL**) project for all your shared code. This is a special project type that allows multiple platforms to reference the same project, allowing you to use the smallest subset of C# and the .NET framework available in each platform. Each platform-specific project would reference this library directly, as well as any unit test projects:
  - **Advantages**: All your shared code is in one project, and all platforms use the same library. Since preprocessor statements aren't possible, PCL libraries generally have cleaner code. Platform specific code is generally abstracted away by interfaces or abstract classes.
  - **Disadvantages**: You are limited to a subset of .NET depending on how many platforms you are targeting. Platform specific code requires use of **dependency injection**, which can be a more advanced topic for developers not familiar with it.

Setting up a shared project

To understand each option completely and what situations call for, let's define a solution structure for both shared projects and portable class libraries. Let's use the product search example from earlier in the chapter and set up a solution for each approach.

To set up a shared project, perform the following steps:

1. Open Xamarin Studio and start a new solution.
2. Select a new **Single View App** under the **Multiplatform | App** section.
3. Name the app `ProductSearch`, and select **Use Shared Library**.
4. Complete this new project wizard and Xamarin Studio will generate three projects: `ProductSearch`, `ProductSearch.Droid`, and `ProductSearch.iOS`.
5. Add the `Product`, `ProductRepository`, and `ProductViewModel` classes to the `ProductSearch` project from earlier in this chapter. You will need to add `using System.Threading.Tasks;` and `using System.Linq;` where needed.
6. Click on **Build | Build All** from the menu at the top to double-check everything, and you have successfully set up a cross-platform solution.

When all is done, you will have a solution tree that looks something like what you can see in the following screenshot:

Shared projects are a great place to start when getting started with cross-platform development. You can't go wrong with them, and they give you ultimate flexibility with the ability to use `#if` throughout your shared code. The only times shared projects might not be the best fit would be if you need to distribute the shared project to others or have a very large team or code base. Preprocessor directives can definitely get out of hand if left unchecked.

In Visual Studio, the project template for a cross-platform application can be found under **Cross-platform | Blank App (Native Shared)**. One thing to note is that it will also generate a Windows Phone project, which you can simply remove if not needed.

Working with portable class libraries

A **portable class library** (PCL) is a C# library project that is able to be supported on multiple platforms including iOS, Android, Windows, Windows Store apps, Windows phone, Silverlight, and Xbox 360. PCLs have been an effort by Microsoft to simplify development across different versions of the .NET framework. Xamarin has also added support on iOS and Android for PCLs. Many popular cross-platform frameworks and open source libraries are starting to develop PCL versions such as Json.NET and MVVMCross.

To set up a shared project, perform the following steps:

1. Open Xamarin Studio and start a new solution.
2. Select a new **Single View App** under the **Multiplatform | App** section. Or in Visual Studio, **Cross-platform | Blank App (Native Portable)**.
3. Name the app `ProductSearch`, and select **Use Portable Library**.
4. Complete this new project wizard and Xamarin Studio will generate three projects: `ProductSearch`, `ProductSearch.Droid`, and `ProductSearch.iOS`.
5. Add the `Product`, `ProductRepository`, and `ProductViewModel` classes to the `ProductSearch` project from earlier in the chapter. You will need to add `using System.Threading.Tasks;` and `using System.Linq;` where needed.
6. Click on **Build | Build All** from the menu at the top to double-check everything, and you have successfully set up a PCL cross-platform solution.

PCLs are the way to go if you need to share your project as a DLL or NuGet package. It also helps you keep platform-specific concerns separate as it forces you to use an interface or base class along with **Dependency Injection (DI)**. Similar issues would arise if you needed to use a native library such as the Facebook SDK on iOS or Android.

 At the time of writing, Microsoft has just released .NET Core and the new .NET Standard. This will affect the way PCLs work in the future, but should not break existing Xamarin.iOS and Xamarin.Android projects. It will, however, enable you to share code with .NET Core and ASP.NET Core projects going forward.

Using preprocessor statements

When using shared projects, one of your most powerful tools is the use of preprocessor statements. If you are unfamiliar with them, C# has the ability to define preprocessor variables such as `#define IPHONE`, and then using `#if IPHONE` or `#if !IPHONE`.

The following is a simple example of using the technique:

```
#if IPHONE
  Console.WriteLine("I am running on iOS");
#elif ANDROID
  Console.WriteLine("I am running on Android");
#else
  Console.WriteLine("I am running on ???");
#endif
```

In Xamarin Studio, you can define preprocessor variables in your project's options under **Build** | **Compiler** | **Define Symbols**, delimited with semicolons. These will be applied to the entire project. Be warned that you must set up these variables for each configuration setting in your solution (**Debug** and **Release**); it can be an easy step to miss. You can also define these variables at the top of any C# file by declaring `#define IPHONE`, but they will only be applied within the C# file.

Let's go over another example, assuming we want to implement a class to open URLs on each platform:

```
public static class Utility
{
  public static void OpenUrl(string url)
  {
    //Open the url in the native browser
  }
}
```

The preceding example is a perfect candidate for using preprocessor statements, since it is very specific to each platform and is a fairly simple function. To implement the method on iOS and Android, we will need to take advantage of some native APIs. Refactor the class to look as follows:

```
#if IPHONE
  //iOS using statements
  using MonoTouch.Foundation;
  using MonoTouch.UIKit;
#elif ANDROID
  //Android using statements
  using Android.App;
```

```
  using Android.Content;
  using Android.Net;
#else
  //Standard .Net using statement
  using System.Diagnostics;
#endif

public static class Utility
{
  #if ANDROID
    public static void OpenUrl(Activity activity, string url)
  #else
    public static void OpenUrl(string url)
  #endif
  {
    //Open the url in the native browser
    #if IPHONE
      UIApplication.SharedApplication.OpenUrl(
        NSUrl.FromString(url));
    #elif ANDROID
      var intent = new Intent(Intent.ActionView,
        Uri.Parse(url));
      activity.StartActivity(intent);
    #else
      Process.Start(url);
    #endif
  }
}
```

The preceding class supports three different types of projects: Android, iOS, and a standard Mono or .NET framework class library. In the case of iOS, we can perform the functionality with static classes available in Apple's APIs. Android is a little more problematic, and requires an `Activity` object for launching a browser natively. We get around this by modifying the input parameters on Android. Lastly, we have a plain .NET version that uses `Process.Start()` to launch a URL. It is important to note that using the third option would not work on iOS or Android natively, which necessitates our use of preprocessor statements.

Using preprocessor statements is not normally the cleanest or the best solution for cross-platform development. They are generally best used in a tight spot or for very simple functions. Code can easily get out of hand and can become very difficult to read with many `#if` statements, so it is always better to use it in moderation. Using inheritance or interfaces is generally a better solution when a class is mostly platform specific.

Simplifying dependency injection

Dependency injection at first seems like a complex topic, but for the most part it is a simple concept. It is a design pattern aimed at making your code within your applications more flexible so that you can swap out certain functionality when needed. The idea builds around setting up dependencies between classes in an application so that each class only interacts with an interface or base/abstract class. This gives you the freedom to override different methods on each platform when you need to fill in native functionality.

The concept originated from the **SOLID** object-oriented design principles, which is a set of rules you might want to research if you are interested in software architecture. The **D** in SOLID stands for **dependencies**. Specifically, the principle declares that a program should depend upon abstractions, not concretions (concrete types).

To build upon this concept, let's walk through the following example:

1. Let's assume we need to store a setting in an application that determines if the sound is on or off.
2. Now let's declare a simple interface for the setting: `interface ISettings { bool IsSoundOn { get; set; } }`.
3. On iOS, we'd want to implement this interface using the `NSUserDefaults` class.
4. Likewise, on Android, we would implement this using `SharedPreferences`.
5. Finally, any class that needs to interact with this setting would only reference `ISettings` so that the implementation could be replaced on each platform.

For reference, the full implementation of this example would look like the following snippet:

```
public interface ISettings
{
  bool IsSoundOn
  {
    get;
    set;
  }
}

//On iOS
using UIKit;
using Foundation;

public class AppleSettings : ISettings
{
  public bool IsSoundOn
```

```
    {
      get
      {
        return NSUserDefaults.StandardUserDefaults
          .BoolForKey("IsSoundOn");
      }
      set
      {
        var defaults = NSUserDefaults.StandardUserDefaults;
        defaults.SetBool(value, "IsSoundOn");
        defaults.Synchronize();
      }
    }
  }

//On Android
using Android.Content;

public class DroidSettings : ISettings
{
  private readonly ISharedPreferences preferences;

  public DroidSettings(Context context)
  {
    preferences = context.GetSharedPreferences(
        context.PackageName, FileCreationMode.Private);
  }

  public bool IsSoundOn
  {
    get
    {
      return preferences.GetBoolean("IsSoundOn", true);
    }
    set
    {
      using (var editor = preferences.Edit())
      {
        editor.PutBoolean("IsSoundOn", value);
        editor.Commit();
      }
    }
  }
}
```

Now you would potentially have a `ViewModel` class that would only reference `ISettings` when following the MVVM pattern. It can be seen in the following snippet:

```
public class SettingsViewModel
{
  private readonly ISettings settings;

  public SettingsViewModel(ISettings settings)
  {
    this.settings = settings;
  }

  public bool IsSoundOn
  {
    get;
    set;
  }

  public void Save()
  {
    settings.IsSoundOn = IsSoundOn;
  }
}
```

Using a ViewModel layer for such a simple example is not necessarily needed, but you can see it would be useful if you needed to perform other tasks such as input validation. A complete application might have a lot more settings and might need to present the user with a loading indicator. Abstracting out your setting's implementation has other benefits that add flexibility to your application. Let's say you suddenly need to replace `NSUserDefaults` on iOS with an iCloud version instead; you can easily do so by implementing a new `ISettings` class and the remainder of your code will remain unchanged. This will also help you target new platforms such as Windows UWP, where you may choose to implement `ISettings` in a platform-specific way.

Implementing Inversion of Control

You might be asking yourself at this point of time, how do I switch out different classes such as the `ISettings` example? **Inversion of Control** (**IoC**) is a design pattern meant to complement the dependency injection and solve this problem. The basic principle is that many of the objects created throughout your application are managed and created by a single class. Instead of using the standard C# constructors for your `ViewModel` or `Model` classes, a service locator or factory class would manage them throughout the application.

There are many different implementations and styles of IoC, so let's implement a simple service locator class to use throughout the remainder of this book as follows:

```
public static class ServiceContainer
{
  static readonly Dictionary<Type, Lazy<object>> services =
    new Dictionary<Type, Lazy<object>>();

  public static void Register<T>(Func<T> function)
  {
    services[typeof(T)] = new Lazy<object>(() => function());
  }

  public static T Resolve<T>()
  {
    return (T)Resolve(typeof(T));
  }

  public static object Resolve(Type type)
  {
    Lazy<object> service;
    if (services.TryGetValue(type, out service))
    {
      return service.Value;
    }
    throw new Exception("Service not found!");
  }
}
```

This class is inspired by the simplicity of XNA/MonoGame's `GameServiceContainer` class, and follows the **service locator** pattern. The main differences are the use of generics and the fact that it is a static class.

To use our `ServiceContainer` class, we would declare the version of `ISettings` or other interfaces that we want to use throughout our application by calling `Register`, as seen in the following lines of code:

```
//iOS version of ISettings
ServiceContainer.Register<ISettings>(() =>
  new AppleSettings());

//Android version of ISettings
ServiceContainer.Register<ISettings>(() =>
  new DroidSettings(this));

//You can even register ViewModels
ServiceContainer.Register<SettingsViewModel>(() =>
```

```
     new SettingsViewModel());
```

On iOS, you could place this registration code in either your `static void Main()` method or in the `FinishedLaunching` method of your `AppDelegate` class. These methods are always called before the application is started.

On Android, it is a little more complicated. You cannot put this code in the `OnCreate` method of your activity that is acting as the main launcher. In some situations, the Android OS can close your application, but restart it later in another activity. This situation would cause your application to crash, as it would try to access services from our container that was not registered yet. The guaranteed safe place to put this is in a custom Android `Application` class, which has an `OnCreate` method that is called prior to any activities being created in your application. The following lines of code show the use of the `Application` class:

```
[Application]
public class Application : Android.App.Application
{
  //This constructor is required
  public Application(IntPtr javaReference, JniHandleOwnership
      transfer): base(javaReference, transfer)
  {

  }

  public override void OnCreate()
  {
    base.OnCreate();

    //IoC Registration here
  }
}
```

To pull a service out of the `ServiceContainer` class, we could rewrite the constructor of the `SettingsViewModel` class, as shown in the following lines of code:

```
public SettingsViewModel()
{
  this.settings = ServiceContainer.Resolve<ISettings>();
}
```

Likewise, you would use the generic `Resolve` method to pull out any `ViewModel` classes you would need to call from within controllers on iOS or activities on Android. This is a great, simple way to manage dependencies within your application.

There are, of course, some great open source libraries out there that implement IoC for C# applications. You might consider switching to one of them if you need more advanced features for service location, or just want to graduate to a more complicated IoC container.

Here are a few libraries that have been used with Xamarin projects:

- **TinyIoC**: `https://github.com/grumpydev/TinyIoC`
- **Ninject**: `http://www.ninject.org/`
- **MvvmCross**: `https://github.com/MvvmCross/MvvmCross` includes a full MVVM framework as well as IoC
- **Autofac**: `https://autofac.org`

Summary

In this chapter, we learned about the MVVM design pattern and how it can be used to better architect cross-platform applications. We compared several project organization strategies for managing a Xamarin Studio solution containing both iOS and Android projects. We went over portable class libraries as the preferred option for sharing code and how to use preprocessor statements as a quick and dirty way to implement platform-specific code.

After completing this chapter, you should be up to speed with several techniques for sharing code between iOS and Android applications using Xamarin Studio. Using the MVVM design pattern will help you separate your shared code and code that is platform specific. We also covered several options for setting up cross-platform Xamarin solutions. You should also have a firm understanding of using the dependency injection and Inversion of Control to give your shared code access to the native APIs on each platform. In our next chapter, we will begin with writing a cross-platform application and dive into using these techniques.

4
XamSnap - A Cross-Platform App

The best way to truly learn a programming skill, in my opinion, is to take on a simple project that requires you to exercise that skill. This gives new developers a project where they can focus on the concepts they are trying to learn without the overhead of fixing bugs or following customer requirements. To increase our understanding of Xamarin and cross-platform development, let's develop a simple app called XamSnap for iOS and Android.

In this chapter, we will cover the following topics:

- Our sample application concept
- The Model layer of our application
- Mocking a web service
- The ViewModel layer of our application
- Writing unit tests

Starting our sample application concept

The concept is simple: a simple clone of the popular chat application, Snapchat. There are several popular applications like this in the Apple App Store, probably due to the cost of text messaging and support for devices such as the iPod Touch or iPad. This should be a neat real-world example that could be useful for users, and will cover specific topics in developing applications for iOS and Android.

Before starting with the development, let's list the set of screens that we'll need:

- **Login / sign up**: This screen will include a standard login and sign-up process for the user.
- **List of conversations**: This screen will include a button to start a new conversation.
- **List of friends**: This screen will provide a way to add new friends when we start a new conversation.
- **Conversation**: This screen will have a list of messages between you and another user, and an option to reply.

- **Camera**: In addition to text messages, Snapchat has the ability to send photos. We will add the option to use the device's camera or photo library for sending photos.

So a quick wireframe layout of the application would help us grasp a better understanding of the layout of the app. The following figure shows the set of screens to be included in your app:

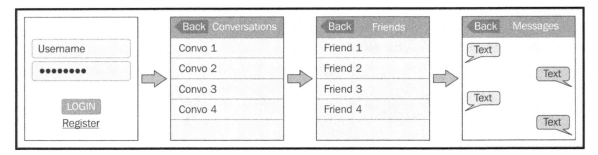

Developing our model layer

Since we have a good idea of what the application is, the next step is to develop the business objects or model layer of this application. Let's start out by defining a few classes that would contain the data to be used throughout the app. It is recommended, for the sake of organization, to add these to a `Models` folder in your project.

Let's begin with a class representing a user. The class can be created as follows:

```
public class User
{
  //NOTE: we will treat this as a unique name
  public string Name { get; set; }

  //NOTE: we'll try to use this in a secure way
  public string Password { get; set; }
}
```

Pretty straightforward so far; let's move on to create classes representing a conversation and a message as follows:

```
public class Conversation
{
  public string Id { get; set; }

  public string UserName { get; set; }
}

public class Message
{
  public string Id { get; set; }

  //NOTE: the Id of a Conversation
  public string Conversation { get; set; }

  public string UserName { get; set; }

  public string Text { get; set; }

//NOTE: some messages will include photos
  public string Image { get; set; }
}
```

Notice that we are using strings as identifiers for the various objects; this will simplify our integration with a backend running as an Azure Function in later chapters. UserName is the value that would be set by the application to change the user that the object is associated with.

Now let's go ahead and set up our solution by performing the following steps:

1. Start by creating a new solution as a new **Multiplatform | App | Single View App** project for iOS and Android.
2. Name the project XamSnap and make sure **Use Portable Class Library** is selected.
3. You could also choose to use a **Shared Project** for this project, but I've chosen to use a portable class library instead.
4. Click **Create** to create your solution in the designated directory.

 Just as in previous chapters, the steps for Visual Studio are a bit different. You will need to create a solution as a Portable Class Library, and *then* add the iOS and Android projects. Do not forget to add a reference to the PCL in both the iOS and Android projects.

Writing a mock web service

Many times when developing a mobile application, you may need to begin the development of your application before the real backend web service is available. To prevent the development from halting entirely, a good approach would be to develop a mock version of the service. This is also helpful when you need to write unit tests, or are waiting on another team to develop the backend for your app.

First, let's break down the operations our app will perform against a web server. The operations are as follows:

1. Login with a username and password.
2. Register a new account.
3. Get the user's list of friends.
4. Add friends by their usernames.
5. Get a list of the existing conversations for the user.
6. Get a list of messages in a conversation.
7. Send a message.

Now let's define an interface that offers a method for each scenario. The method is as follows:

```
public interface IWebService
{
    Task<User> Login(string userName, string password);
```

```
    Task<User> Register(User user);

    Task<User[]> GetFriends(string userName);

    Task<User> AddFriend(string username, string friendName);

    Task<Conversation[]> GetConversations(string userName);

    Task<Message[]> GetMessages(string conversation);

    Task<Message> SendMessage(Message message);
}
```

As you see, we're simplifying any asynchronous communication with a web service by leveraging the **TPL (Task Parallel Library)** from the .NET base class libraries.

Since communicating with a web service can be a lengthy process, it is always a good idea to use the `Task<T>` class for these operations. Otherwise, you could inadvertently run a lengthy task on the user interface thread, which would prevent user inputs during the operation. `Task` is definitely needed for web requests, since users could easily be using a cellular Internet connection on iOS and Android, and it will give us the ability to use the `async` and `await` keywords down the road.

> If you are not familiar with async/await for simplified asynchronous programming in C#, it would be helpful to review the subject on MSDN at: https://msdn.microsoft.com/en-us/library/mt674882.aspx

Now let's implement a **fake** service that implements this interface. Place classes such as `FakeWebService` in the `Fakes` folder of the project. Let's start with the class declaration and the first method of the interface:

```
public class FakeWebService : IWebService
{
  public int SleepDuration { get; set; }

  public FakeWebService()
  {
    SleepDuration = 1000;
  }

  private Task Sleep()
  {
    return Task.Delay(SleepDuration);
  }
```

```
    public async Task<User> Login(string userName, string password)
    {
      await Sleep();
      return new User { Name = userName };
    }
}
```

We started off with a `SleepDuration` property to store a number in milliseconds. This is used to simulate an interaction with a web server, which can take some time. It is also useful for changing the `SleepDuration` value in different situations. For example, you might want to set this to a small number when writing unit tests so that the tests execute quickly.

Next, we implemented a simple `Sleep` method to return a task that introduces a delay of a number of milliseconds. This method will be used throughout the fake service to cause a delay on each operation.

Finally, the `Login` method merely used an `await` call on the `Sleep` method and returned a new `User` object with the appropriate `Name`. For now, any username or password combination will work; however, you may wish to write some code here to check specific credentials.

Now, let's implement a few more methods to continue our `FakeWebService` class as follows:

```
public async Task<User[]> GetFriends(string userId)
{
  await Sleep();
  return new[]
  {
    new User { Name = "bobama" },
    new User { Name = "bobloblaw" },
    new User { Name = "georgemichael" },
  };
}

public async Task<User> AddFriend(
  string username, string friendName)
{
  await Sleep();
  return new User { Name = friendName };
}
```

For each of these methods, we kept in mind exactly the same pattern as the `Login` method. Each method will delay and return some sample data. Feel free to mix up the data with your own values.

Now, let's implement the `GetConversations` method required by the interface as follows:

```
public async Task<Conversation[]> GetConversations(
  string userName)
{
  await Sleep();
  return new[]
  {
    new Conversation { Id = "1", UserName = "bobama" },
    new Conversation { Id = "2", UserName = "bobloblaw" },
    new Conversation { Id = "3", UserName = "georgemichael" },
  };
}
```

Basically, we just create a new array of the `Conversation` objects with arbitrary IDs. We also make sure to match up the `UserName` values with what we used on the `User` objects so far.

Next, let's implement `GetMessages` to retrieve a list of messages as follows:

```
public async Task<Message[]> GetMessages(string conversation)
{
  await Sleep();

  return new[]
  {
    new Message
    {
      Id = "1",
      Conversation = conversation,
      UserName = "bobloblaw",
      Text = "Hey",
    },
    new Message
    {
      Id = "2",
      Conversation = conversation,
      UserName = "georgemichael",
      Text = "What's Up?",
    },
    new Message
    {
      Id = "3",
```

```
      Conversation = conversation,
      UserName = "bobloblaw",
      Text = "Have you seen that new movie?",
    },
    new Message
    {
      Id = "4",
      Conversation = conversation,
      UserName = "georgemichael",
      Text = "It's great!",
    },
  };
}
```

Once again, we are adding some arbitrary data here, and mainly making sure that `UserId` and `ConversationId` match our existing data so far.

And finally, we will write one more method to send a message as follows:

```
public async Task<Message> SendMessage(Message message)
{
  await Sleep();

  return message;
}
```

Most of these methods are very straightforward. Note that the service doesn't have to work perfectly; it should merely complete each operation successfully with a delay. Each method should also return test data of some kind to be displayed in the UI. This will give us the ability to implement our iOS and Android applications while filling in the web service later.

Next, we need to implement a simple interface for persisting application settings. Let's define an interface named `ISettings` as follows:

```
public interface ISettings
{
  User User { get; set; }

  void Save();
}
```

We are making `ISettings` synchronous, but you might want to set up the `Save` method to be asynchronous and return `Task` if you plan on storing settings in the cloud. We don't really need this with our application since we will only be saving our settings locally.

Later on, we'll implement this interface on each platform using Android and iOS APIs. For now, let's just implement a fake version that will be used later when we write unit tests. Implement the interface with the following lines of code:

```
public class FakeSettings : ISettings
{
  public User User { get; set; }

  public void Save() { }
}
```

Note that the fake version doesn't actually need to do anything; we just need to provide a class that will implement the interface and not throw any unexpected errors.

This completes the Model layer of the application. Here is a final class diagram of what we have implemented so far:

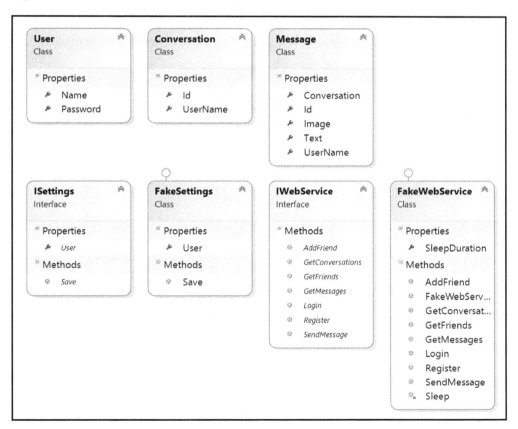

Writing the ViewModel layer

Now that we have our model layer implemented, we can move on to write the ViewModel layer. The ViewModel will be responsible for presenting each operation to the UI and offering properties to be filled out by the View layer. Other common responsibilities of this layer are input validation and simple logic to display busy indicators.

At this point, it would be a good idea to include the `ServiceContainer` class from the previous chapter in our `XamSnap` PCL project, as we will be using it through our ViewModels to interact with the Model layer. We will be using it as a simple option to support dependency injection and Inversion of Control; however, you may use another library of your preference for this.

Normally, we start off by writing a base class for all the ViewModel layers within our project. It's a good place to put some parts of the code that are used by all the subclasses, for example: notification changes, methods, or commonly used interfaces.

Place the following code snippet in a new `ViewModels` folder within your project:

```
public class BaseViewModel
{
  protected readonly IWebService service =
    ServiceContainer.Resolve<IWebService>();
  protected readonly ISettings settings =
    ServiceContainer.Resolve<ISettings>();

  public event EventHandler IsBusyChanged = (sender, e) => { };

  private bool isBusy = false;

  public bool IsBusy
  {
    get { return isBusy; }
    set
    {
      isBusy = value;
      IsBusyChanged(this, EventArgs.Empty);
    }
  }
}
```

The `BaseViewModel` class is a great place to place any common functionality that you plan on reusing throughout your application. For this app, we only need to implement a way to indicate if the ViewModel layer is busy. We provided a property and an event that the UI will be able to subscribe to and display a wait indicator on the screen. We also added some fields for the services that will be needed. Another common feature that could be added would be validation for user inputs; however, we don't really need it for this application.

Implementing our LoginViewModel class

Now that we have a base class for all of the ViewModel layers, we can implement ViewModel for the first screen in our application, the **Login** screen.

Now let's implement a `LoginViewModel` class as follows:

```
public class LoginViewModel : BaseViewModel
{
  public string UserName { get; set; }

  public string Password { get; set; }

  public async Task Login()
  {
    if (string.IsNullOrEmpty(UserName))
      throw new Exception("Username is blank.");

    if (string.IsNullOrEmpty(Password))
      throw new Exception("Password is blank.");

    IsBusy = true;
    try
    {
      settings.User = await service.Login(UserName, Password);
      settings.Save();
    }
    finally
    {
      IsBusy = false;
    }
  }
}
```

In this class, we implemented the following:

- We subclassed `BaseViewModel` to get access to `IsBusy` and the fields containing common services
- We added the `UserName` and `Password` properties to be set by the View layer
- We added a `User` property to be set when the log in process is completed
- We implemented a `Login` method to be called from View, with validation on `UserName` and `Password` properties
- We set `IsBusy` during the call to the `Login` method on `IWebService`
- We set the `User` property by awaiting the result from `Login` on the web service

Basically, this is the pattern that we'll follow for the rest of the ViewModels in the application. We provide properties for the View layer to be set by the user's input, and methods to call for various operations. If it is a method that could take some time, such as a web request, you should always return `Task` and use the `async` and `await` keywords.

Note that we used a `try` and `finally` block for setting `IsBusy` back to `false`. This will ensure it gets reset properly even when an exception is thrown. We plan on handling the error in the View layer, so we can display a native popup to the user displaying a message.

Implementing our RegisterViewModel class

Since we have finished writing our `ViewModel` class to log in, we will now need to create one for the user's registration.

Let's implement another ViewModel to register a new user:

```
public class RegisterViewModel : BaseViewModel
{
  public string UserName { get; set; }

  public string Password { get; set; }

  public string ConfirmPassword { get; set; }
}
```

These properties will handle inputs from the user. Next, we need to add a `Register` method as follows:

```
public async Task Register()
{
```

```
    if (string.IsNullOrEmpty(UserName))
      throw new Exception("Username is blank.");

    if (string.IsNullOrEmpty(Password))
      throw new Exception("Password is blank.");

    if (Password != ConfirmPassword)
      throw new Exception("Passwords do not match.");

    IsBusy = true;
    try
    {
      settings.User = await service.Register(new User
      {
        Name = UserName,
        Password = Password,
      });
      settings.Save();
    }
    finally
    {
      IsBusy = false;
    }
  }
```

The `RegisterViewModel` class is very similar to the `LoginViewModel` class, but it has an additional `ConfirmPassword` property for the UI to set. A good rule to follow for when to split up the ViewModel layer's functionality is to always create a new class when the UI has a new screen. This helps to keep your code clean and somewhat follow the **single responsibility principle** for your classes. The **SRP** states that a class should only have a single purpose or responsibility. We'll try to follow this concept to keep our classes small and organized, which can be more important than usual when sharing code across platforms.

Implementing our FriendViewModel class

Next on the list is a ViewModel layer to work with a user's friend list. We will need a method to load a user's friend list and add a new friend.

Now let's implement the `FriendViewModel` as follows:

```
public class FriendViewModel : BaseViewModel
{
  public User[] Friends { get; private set; }
```

```
    public string UserName { get; set; }
  }
```

Now we'll need a method to load friends. This method is as follows:

```
public async Task GetFriends()
{
  if (settings.User == null)
    throw new Exception("Not logged in.");

  IsBusy = true;
  try
  {
    Friends = await service.GetFriends(settings.User.Name);
  }
  finally
  {
    IsBusy = false;
  }
}
```

Finally, we'll need a method to add a new friend, and then update the list of friends contained locally:

```
public async Task AddFriend()
{
  if (settings.User == null)
    throw new Exception("Not logged in.");
  if (string.IsNullOrEmpty(UserName))
    throw new Exception("Username is blank.");
  IsBusy = true;

  try
  {
    var friend = await service
      .AddFriend(settings.User.Name, UserName);
    //Update our local list of friends
    var friends = new List<User>();
    if (Friends != null)
      friends.AddRange(Friends);
    friends.Add(friend);
    Friends =  friends.OrderBy(f => f.Name).ToArray();
  }
  finally
  {
    IsBusy =  false;
  }
}
```

Again, this class is fairly straightforward. The only thing new here is that we added some logic to update the list of friends and sort them within our client application and not the server. You could also choose to reload the complete list of friends if you have a good reason to do so.

Implementing our MessageViewModel class

Our final required ViewModel layer will be handling messages and conversations. We need to create a way to load conversations and messages, and send a new message.

Let's start implementing our MessageViewModel class as follows:

```
public class MessageViewModel : BaseViewModel
{
  public Conversation[] Conversations { get; private set; }

  public Conversation Conversation { get; set; }

  public Message[] Messages { get; private set; }

  public string Text { get; set; }
}
```

Next, let's implement a method to retrieve a list of conversations as follows:

```
public async Task GetConversations()
{
  if (settings.User == null)
    throw new Exception("Not logged in.");

  IsBusy = true;
  try
  {
    Conversations = await service
        .GetConversations(settings.User.Name);
  }
  finally
  {
    IsBusy = false;
  }
}
```

Similarly, we need to retrieve a list of messages within a conversation. We will need to pass the conversation ID to the service as follows:

```
public async Task GetMessages()
{
  if (Conversation == null)
    throw new Exception("No conversation.");

  IsBusy = true;
  try
  {
    Messages = await service
      .GetMessages(Conversation.Id);
  }
  finally
  {
    IsBusy = false;
  }
}
```

Finally, we need to write some code to send a message and update the local list of messages as follows:

```
public async Task SendMessage()
{
  if (settings.User == null)
    throw new Exception("Not logged in.");

  if (Conversation == null)
    throw new Exception("No conversation.");

  if (string.IsNullOrEmpty (Text))
    throw new Exception("Message is blank.");

  IsBusy = true;
  try
  {
    var message = await service.SendMessage(new Message
    {
        UserName = settings.User.Name,
         Conversation = Conversation.Id,
        Text = Text
    });

    //Update our local list of messages
    var messages = new List<Message>();
    if (Messages != null)
      messages.AddRange(Messages);
```

```
    messages.Add(message);

    Messages = messages.ToArray();
  }
  finally
  {
    IsBusy = false;
  }
}
```

This concludes the ViewModel layer of our application and the entirety of the shared code used on iOS and Android. For the `MessageViewModel` class, you could have also chosen to put `GetConversations` and `Conversations` properties in their own class, since they could be considered as a separate responsibility, but it is not really necessary.

Here is the final class diagram of our ViewModel layer:

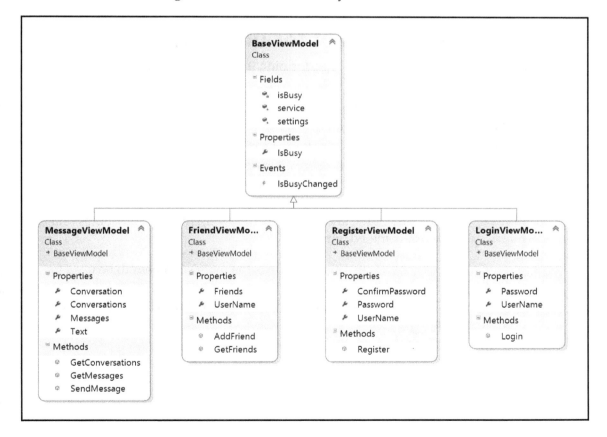

Writing unit tests

Since all the code we've written so far is not dependent on the user interface, we can easily write unit tests against our classes. This step is generally taken after the first implementation of a `ViewModel` class. Proponents of **Test Driven Development (TDD)** would recommend writing tests first and implementing things afterward, so choose which method is best for you. In either case, it is a good idea to write tests against your shared code before you start using them from the View layer, so you catch bugs before they hold up your development on the UI.

Xamarin projects take advantage of an open source testing framework called **NUnit**. It was originally derived from a Java testing framework called **JUnit**, and is the de-facto standard for unit testing C# applications. Xamarin Studio provides several project templates for writing tests with **NUnit**.

Setting up a new project for unit tests

Let's set up a new project for unit tests by performing the following steps:

1. Add a new **NUnit Library Project** to your solution, found under the **Other | .Net** section in Xamarin Studio. If using Visual Studio, create a .NET class library and add the NUnit NuGet package.
2. Name the project as `XamSnap.Tests` to keep things consistent.
3. Right-click on the project references and choose **Edit References**.
4. Under the **Projects** tab, add a reference to **XamSnap**, your existing portable class library.
5. Now, open the `Test.cs` file and notice the following required attributes that make up a unit test using NUnit:

   - `using NUnit.Framework`: This attribute is the main statement to be used to work with NUnit
   - `[TestFixture]`: This decorates a class to indicate that the class has a list of methods for running tests
   - `[Test]`: This decorates a method to indicate a test

In addition to the required C# attributes, there are several others that are useful for writing tests and they are as follows:

- `[TestFixtureSetUp]`: This decorates a method that runs before all the tests contained within a text fixture class.
- `[SetUp]`: This decorates a method that runs before each test in a test fixture class.
- `[TearDown]`: This decorates a method that runs after each test in a test fixture class.
- `[TestFixtureTearDown]`: This decorates a method that runs after all the tests in a text fixture class have been completed.
- `[ExpectedException]`: This decorates a method that is intended to throw an exception. It is useful to test cases that are supposed to fail.
- `[Category]`: This decorates a test method and can be used to organize different tests; for example, you might categorize fast and slow tests.

Writing assertions

The next concept to learn about writing tests with NUnit is learning how to write **assertions**. An assertion is a method that will throw an exception if a certain value is not true. It will cause a test to fail and give a descriptive explanation as to what happened. NUnit has a couple of different sets of APIs for assertions; however, we will use the more readable and fluent version of the APIs.

The basic syntax of fluent-style API is using the `Assert.That` method. The following example shows the this:

```
Assert.That(myVariable, Is.EqualTo(0));
```

Likewise, you can assert the opposite:

```
Assert.That(myVariable, Is.Not.EqualTo(0));
```

Or any of the following:

- Assert.That(myVariable, Is.GreaterThan(0));
- Assert.That(myBooleanVariable, Is.True);
- Assert.That(myObject, Is.Not.Null);

Feel free to explore the APIs. With code completion in Xamarin Studio, you should be able to discover useful static members or methods on the `Is` class to use within your tests.

Before we begin writing specific tests for our application, let's write a static class and method to create a global setup to be used throughout our tests; you can rewrite `Test.cs` as follows:

```
public class BaseTest
{
  [SetUp]
  public virtual void SetUp()
  {
    ServiceContainer.Register<IWebService>(() =>
        new FakeWebService { SleepDuration = 0 });
    ServiceContainer.Register<ISettings>(() =>
        new FakeSettings());
  }
}
```

We'll use this method throughout our tests to set up fake services in our Model layer. Additionally, this replaces the existing services so that our tests execute against new instances of these classes. This is a good practice in unit testing to guarantee that no old data is left behind from a previous test. Also notice that we set `SleepDuration` to 0. This will make our tests run very quickly.

Begin by creating a `ViewModels` folder in your test's project and adding a class named `LoginViewModelTests` as follows:

```
[TestFixture]
public class LoginViewModelTests : BaseTest
{
  LoginViewModel loginViewModel;
  ISettings settings;

  [SetUp]
  public override void SetUp()
  {
    base.SetUp();

    settings = ServiceContainer.Resolve<ISettings>();
    loginViewModel = new LoginViewModel();
  }

  [Test]
  public async Task LoginSuccessfully()
  {
    loginViewModel.UserName = "testuser";
```

```
    loginViewModel.Password = "password";

    await loginViewModel.Login();

    Assert.That(settings.User, Is.Not.Null);
    }
  }
```

Notice our use of a `SetUp` method. We recreate the objects used in every test to make sure that no old data is left over from the previous test runs. Another point to note is that you must return a `Task` when using `async/await` in a test method. Otherwise, NUnit would not be able to know when a test completes.

To run the test, use the NUnit menu found docked to the right of Xamarin Studio by default. Go ahead and run the test by using the **Run Test** button that has a gear icon; you should get a successful result similar to what is shown in the following screenshot:

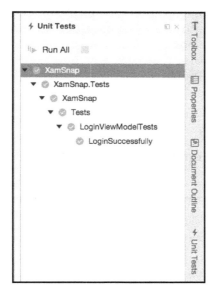

You can also view the **Test Results** pane, which will show extended details if a test fails; as shown in the following screenshot:

If using Visual Studio, you will need to install the **NUnit Test Adapter** extension from the Visual Studio gallery. You can find this option under the **Tools | Extensions and Updates** menu. The unit test runner in Visual Studio is just as intuitive as Xamarin Studio; however, it only supports MsTest out of the box.

To see what happens when a test fails, go ahead and modify your test to assert against an incorrect value as follows:

```
//Change Is.Not.Null to Is.Null
Assert.That(settings.User, Is.Null);
```

You will get a very descriptive error in the **Test Results** pane, as shown in the following screenshot:

Now let's implement another test for the `LoginViewModel` class; let's make sure we get the appropriate outcome if the username and password is blank. The test is implemented as follows:

```
[Test]
public async Task LoginWithNoUsernameOrPassword()
{
  //Throws an exception
  await loginViewModel.Login();
}
```

If we run the test as is, we will get an exception and the test will fail. Since we expect an exception to occur, we can decorate the method to make the test pass only if an exception occurs, as follows:

```
[Test,
  ExpectedException(typeof(Exception),
  ExpectedMessage = "Username is blank.")]
```

> Note that in our view model a generic `Exception` type is thrown if a **field is blank**. You can also change the type of expected exception in cases where it is a different exception type.

More tests are included with the sample code along with this book. It is recommended to write tests against each public operation on each `ViewModel` class. Additionally, write tests for any validation or other important business logic. I would also recommend writing tests against the Model layer; however, it is not needed in our project yet since we only have fake implementations.

Summary

In this chapter, we went over the concept for a sample application that we will be building throughout this book called XamSnap. We also implemented the core business objects for the application in the Model layer. Since we do not have a server to support this application yet, we implemented a fake web service. This gives us the flexibility to move forward with the app without building a server application. We also implemented the ViewModel layer. This layer will expose operations in a simple way to the View layer. Finally, we wrote tests covering the code we've written so far using NUnit. Writing tests against shared code in a cross-platform application can be very important, as it is the backbone of more than one application.

After completing this chapter, you should have completed the shared library for our cross-platform application in its entirety. You should have a very firm grasp on our application's architecture and its distinct Model and ViewModel layers. You should also have a good understanding on how to write fake versions of parts of your application that you may not be ready to implement quite yet. In the next chapter, we will implement the iOS version of XamSnap.

5
XamSnap for iOS

To begin writing the iOS version of XamSnap, open the solution we created in the previous chapter. We will be working mostly in the `XamSnap.iOS` project in this chapter. The project template will have automatically created a controller named `ViewController`; go ahead and delete it. We will create our own controllers as we go.

In this chapter, we will cover the following:

- The basics of an iOS application
- Using UINavigationController
- Implementing a login screen
- Segues and UITableView
- Adding a friends list
- Adding a list of messages
- Composing messages

Understanding the basics of an iOS app

Before we start developing our app, let's review the main settings of the application. Apple uses a file named `Info.plist` to store important information about any iOS app. These settings are used by the OS itself and when an iOS application is installed on a device by the Apple App Store. Begin development of any new iOS application by filling out the information in this file.

Xamarin Studio provides a neat menu to modify values in the `Info.plist` file, as shown in the following screenshot:

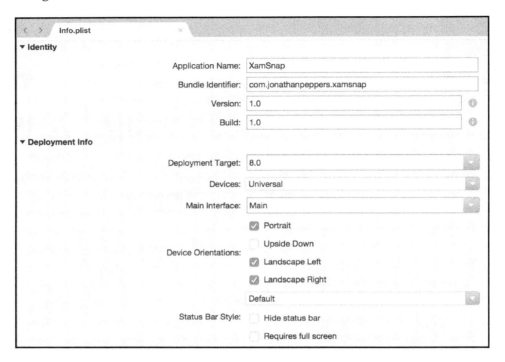

The most important settings are as follows:

- **Application Name**: This is the title below an app's icon in iOS. Note that this is not the same as the official name of your app in the iOS App Store.
- **Bundle Identifier**: This is your app's bundle identifier or bundle ID. It is a unique name to identify your application. The convention is to use a reverse domain naming style beginning with your company name, such as `com.jonathanpeppers.xamsnap`.

- **Version**: This is the version number for your application that is visible to the users on the app store, such as `1.0.0`.
- **Build**: This is the version number reserved for the developer (for CI builds, etc.), such as `1.0.0.1234`.
- **Devices**: In this, you can select **iPhone/iPod**, **iPad**, or **Universal** (all devices) for your application.
- **Deployment Target**: This is the minimum iOS version your application runs on.
- **Main Interface**: This is the main storyboard file for your app.
- **Device Orientations**: These are the different positions your application will be able to rotate to and support.
- **Status Bar Style**: These are the options to hide the top status bar in your application and run full screen.

There are other settings for app icons, splash screens, and so on. You can also toggle between the **Advanced** or **Source** tabs to configure additional settings for which Xamarin does not provide a user-friendly menu.

Configure the following settings for our application:

- **Application Name**: `XamSnap`
- **Bundle Identifier**: `com.yourcompanyname.xamsnap`; make sure you name future apps so that they begin with `com.yourcompanyname`.
- **Devices: iPhone/iPod**
- **Deployment Target**: 8.0
- **Supported Device Orientations**: Only select **Portrait**.

Xamarin.iOS Build Options

You can find some additional settings for Xamarin iOS applications if you right-click on your project and select **Options**, as shown in the following screenshot. It is a good idea to know what is available for iOS-specific projects in Xamarin Studio. A lot is going on here, but the defaults will get you by in most situations.

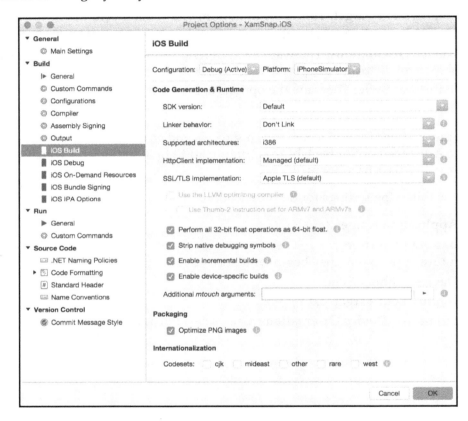

Let's discuss some of the most important options, as follows:

iOS Build

- **SDK version**: This is the version of the iOS SDK to compile your application with. It is generally best to use **Default**.
- **Linker behavior**: Xamarin has implemented a feature called **linking**. The linker will strip any code that will never be called within your assemblies. This keeps your application small, and allows them to ship a stripped-down version of the

core Mono runtime with your app. Except for debug builds, it is best to use the **Link SDK assemblies only** option. We will cover linking in a future chapter.

- **Supported Architectures**: These are the types of processors. `i386` is the simulator and `ARMv7 + ARM64` is the option for compiling for modern iOS devices. You should generally be able to use the defaults here, unless upgrading an older Xamarin.iOS application.

- **HttpClient implementation**: newer versions of Xamarin.iOS allow you to choose a native HTTP stack for `System.Net.Http.HttpClient`. Mono's implementation is the default, but is not as performant as the native stack.

- **SSL/TLS implementation**: Xamarin.iOS also has the option to use native APIs for SSL. If you choose Mono instead, your application will only support TLS 1.0, so it is better to use the native option here.

- **Use LLVM optimizing compiler**: Checking this compiles code that is smaller and runs faster, but takes longer to compile. **LLVM** stands for **Low Level Virtual Machine**.

- **Strip native debugging symbols**: When this option is on, Xamarin removes extra information from your app that would enable debugging from Xamarin Studio.

- **Additional mtouch arguments**: This field is for passing extra command-line arguments to the Xamarin compiler for iOS. You can check the complete list of these arguments at https://developer.xamarin.com/api.

- **Optimize PNG files for iOS**: Apple uses a custom PNG format to speed up the loading of PNGs within your app. You can turn this off to speed up builds, or if you plan on optimizing the images yourself.

iOS Bundle Signing

- **Signing Identity**: This is the certificate to identify the app's creator for deploying the application to devices. We'll cover more on this in later chapters.

- **Provisioning profile**: This is a specific profile that deploys the app to a device. This works in tandem with **Signing Identity**, but also declares the distribution method and the devices that can install the app.

- **Custom Entitlements**: This file contains additional settings to be applied with the provisioning profile and contains other specific declarations for the app, such as iCloud or push notifications. The project template for iOS apps includes a default `Entitlements.plist` file for new projects.

For this application, you can leave all these options at their defaults. When making a real iOS application on your own, you should consider changing many of these as per your application's needs.

Using UINavigationController

In iOS applications, the key class for managing navigation between different controllers is the UINavigationController class. It is a parent controller that contains several child controllers in a stack. Users can move forward by putting new controllers on top of the stack, or using a built-in back button to pop a controller off the stack and navigate to the previous screen.

The developer can manipulate the navigation controller's stack with the following methods:

- SetViewControllers: This sets an array of child controllers. It has a value to optionally animate the transition.
- ViewControllers: This is a property for getting or setting the array of child controllers without an option for animation.
- PushViewController: This places a new child controller at the top of the stack and has an option to display an animation.
- PopViewController: This pops off the child controller at the top of the stack and has an option to animate the transition.
- PopToViewController: This pops to the specified child controller, removing all controllers above it. It provides an option to animate the transition.
- PopToRootViewController: This removes all child controllers except the bottom-most controller. It includes an option to display an animation.
- TopViewController: This is a property that returns the child controller that is currently on top of the stack.

It is important to note that using the option for animations will cause a crash if you try to modify the stack during the animation. To fix this situation, either use the SetViewControllers method and set the entire list of child controllers, or refrain from using the animations during a combination of transitions.

Let's set up a navigation controller in our application by performing the following steps:

1. Double-click on the Main.storyboard file to open it in Xamarin Studio.
2. Remove the controller that was created by the project template.
3. Drag a **Navigation Controller** element from the **Toolbox** on the right onto the storyboard.
4. Notice that a default **View Controller** element was created, as well as a **Navigation Controller**.

5. You will see a **segue** that connects the two controllers. We'll cover this concept in more detail later in the chapter.

6. Save the storyboard file.

Just a note for Visual Studio users, Xamarin has done a great job making their Visual Studio Extension work identically to Xamarin Studio. All of the examples in this chapter should work just as described in either Xamarin Studio on OS X or Visual Studio on Windows. The exception, of course, is a remotely connected mac for deploying to the simulator or an iOS device.

If you run the application at this point, you will have a basic iOS app with a status bar at the top, a navigation controller containing a navigation bar with a default title, and a child controller that is completely white, as shown in the following screenshot:

Implementing the login screen

Since the first screen of our application will be a login screen, let's begin by setting up the appropriate views in the storyboard file. We will implement the login screen by using Xamarin Studio to write the C# code, and its iOS designer to create iOS layouts in our storyboard file.

Return to the project in Xamarin Studio and perform the following steps:

1. Double-click on the `Main.storyboard` file to open it in the iOS designer.
2. Select your view controller, click on the **Properties** pane and select the **Widget** tab.
3. Enter `LoginController` into the **Class** field.
4. Notice that the `LoginController` class is generated for you. You may create a `Controllers` folder and move the file into it if you wish.

The following screenshot shows what the controller's settings will look like in Xamarin Studio after the changes have been made:

Now let's modify the layout of the controller by performing the following steps:

1. Double-click on the `Main.storyboard` file a second time to return to the iOS designer.
2. Tap on the navigation bar and edit the **Title** field to read `Login`.
3. Drag two text fields onto the controller. Position and size them appropriately for the username and password entries. You may also want to remove the default text to make the fields blank.
4. For the second field, check the **Secure Text Entry** checkbox. This will set the control to hide the characters for the password field.

5. You may also want to fill out the **Placeholder** field for `Username` and `Password`.

6. Drag a button onto the controller. Set the button's **Title** to `Login`.

7. Drag an activity indicator onto the controller. Check the **Animating** and **Hidden** checkboxes.

8. Next, create the outlets for each of the controls by filling out the **Name** field. Name the outlets `username`, `password`, `login`, and `indicator`, respectively.

9. Save the storyboard file and take a look at `LoginController.designer.cs`.

You will notice that Xamarin Studio has generated properties for each of the outlets:

```
1  // WARNING
2  //
3  // This file has been generated automatically by Xamarin Studio
4  // actions declared in your storyboard file.
5  // Manual changes to this file will not be maintained.
6  //
7  using Foundation;
8  using System;
9  using System.CodeDom.Compiler;
10 using UIKit;
11
12 namespace XamSnap.iOS
13 {
14     [Register ("LoginController")]
15     partial class LoginController
16     {
17         [Outlet]
18         [GeneratedCode ("iOS Designer", "1.0")]
19         UIKit.UIActivityIndicatorView indicator { get; set; }
20
21         [Outlet]
22         [GeneratedCode ("iOS Designer", "1.0")]
23         UIKit.UIButton login { get; set; }
24
25         [Outlet]
26         [GeneratedCode ("iOS Designer", "1.0")]
27         UIKit.UITextField password { get; set; }
```

Go ahead and compile the application to make sure everything is okay. At this point, we also need to add a reference to the `XamSnap.Core` project created in the previous chapter.

Next, let's set up our iOS application to register all its view models and the other services that will be used throughout the application. We will use the `ServiceContainer` class we created in `Chapter 4`, *XamSnap - A Cross-Platform App*, to set up dependencies throughout our application. Open `AppDelegate.cs` and add the following method:

```
public override bool FinishedLaunching(
    UIApplication application,
    NSDictionary launchOptions)
{
  //View Models
  ServiceContainer.Register<LoginViewModel>(() =>
      new LoginViewModel());
  ServiceContainer.Register<FriendViewModel>(() =>
      new FriendViewModel());
  ServiceContainer.Register<RegisterViewModel>(() =>
      new RegisterViewModel());
  ServiceContainer.Register<MessageViewModel>(() =>
      new MessageViewModel());

  //Models
  ServiceContainer.Register<ISettings>(() =>
      new FakeSettings());
  ServiceContainer.Register<IWebService>(() =>
      new FakeWebService());
  return true;
}
```

Down the road, we will replace the fake services with real ones. Now let's add the login functionality to `LoginController.cs`. First add `LoginViewModel` to a member variable at the top of the class, as follows:

```
readonly LoginViewModel loginViewModel =
    ServiceContainer.Resolve<LoginViewModel>();
```

This will pull a shared instance of `LoginViewModel` into a local variable in the controller. This is the pattern we will use throughout the book in order to pass a shared view model from one class to another.

Next, override `ViewDidLoad` to hook up the view model's functionality with the views set up in outlets, as follows:

```
public override void ViewDidLoad()
{
  base.ViewDidLoad();

  login.TouchUpInside += async(sender, e) =>
  {
```

```
      loginViewModel.UserName = username.Text;
      loginViewModel.Password = password.Text;

      try
      {
        await loginViewModel.Login();

        //TODO: navigate to a new screen
      }
      catch (Exception exc)
      {
        new UIAlertView("Oops!", exc.Message, null, "Ok").Show();
      }
    };
}
```

We'll add the code to navigate to a new screen later in the chapter.

Next, let's hook up the `IsBusyChanged` event to actually perform an action, as follows:

```
public override void ViewWillAppear(bool animated)
{
  base.ViewWillAppear(animated);

  loginViewModel.IsBusyChanged += OnIsBusyChanged;
}

public override void ViewWillDisappear(bool animated)
{
  base.ViewWillDisappear(animated);

  loginViewModel.IsBusyChanged -= OnIsBusyChanged;
}

void OnIsBusyChanged(object sender, EventArgs e)
{
  username.Enabled =
    password.Enabled =
    login.Enabled =
    indicator.Hidden = !loginViewModel.IsBusy;
}
```

Now, you might ask why we subscribe to the event in this manner. The problem is that the `LoginViewModel` class will last through your application's lifetime, while the `LoginController` class will not. If we subscribed to the event in `ViewDidLoad`, but didn't unsubscribe later, then our application would have a memory leak. We also avoided using a lambda expression for the event, since it would otherwise be impossible to unsubscribe to the event.

Note that we don't have the same problem with the `TouchUpInside` event on the button, since it will live in memory as long as the controller does. This is a common problem with events in C#, which is why it is a good idea to use the preceding pattern on iOS.

If you run the application now, you should be able to enter a username and password, as shown in the following screenshot. On pressing **Login**, you should see the indicator appear and all the controls disabled. Your application will correctly be calling the shared code, and should function correctly when we add a real web service.

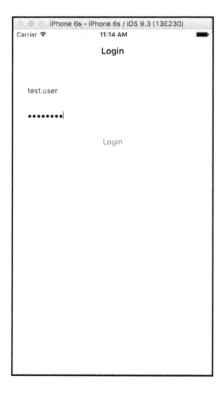

Using segues for navigation

A segue is a transition from one controller to another. In the same way, a storyboard file is a collection of controllers and their views attached together by segues. This, in turn, allows you to see the layouts of each controller and the general flow of your application at the same time.

There are just a few categories of segue, which are as follows:

- **Push**: This is used within a navigation controller. It pushes a new controller to the top of the navigation controller's stack. Push uses the standard animation technique for navigation controllers and is generally the most commonly used segue.
- **Relationship**: This is used to set a child controller for another controller. For example, the root controller of a navigation controller, container views, or split view controllers in an iPad application.
- **Modal**: On using this, a controller presented modally will appear on top of the parent controller. It will cover the entire screen until dismissed. There are several types of different transition animations available.
- **Custom**: This is a custom segue that includes an option for a custom class, which subclasses `UIStoryboardSegue`. This gives you fine-grained control over the animation and how the next controller is presented.

Segues also keep to the following pattern while executing:

- The destination controller and its views are created.
- The segue object, a subclass of `UIStoryboardSegue`, is created. This is normally only important for custom segues.
- The `PrepareForSegue` method is called on the source controller. This is a good place to run any custom code before a segue begins.
- The segue's `Perform` method is called and the transition animation is started. This is where the bulk of the code resides for a custom segue.

In the Xamarin.iOS designer you have the choice of either firing a segue automatically from a button or table view row, or just giving the segue an identifier. In the second case, you can start the segue yourself by calling the `PerformSegue` method on the source controller by using its identifier.

Now let's set up a new segue by setting up some aspects of our `Main.storyboard` file through performing the following steps:

1. Double-click on the `Main.storyboard` file to open it in the iOS designer.
2. Add a new **Table View Controller** to the storyboard.
3. Select your view controller, and navigate to the **Properties** pane and the **Widget** tab.
4. Enter `ConversationsController` into the **Class** field.
5. Scroll down under the **View Controller** section and enter a **Title** of `Conversations`.
6. Create a segue from `LoginController` to `ConversationsController` by clicking while holding Ctrl and dragging the blue line from one controller to the other.
7. Select the **Show** segue from the pop up that appears.
8. Select the segue by clicking on it and give it an **Identifier** of `OnLogin`.
9. Save the storyboard file.

Your storyboard will look something like similar to what is shown in the following screenshot:

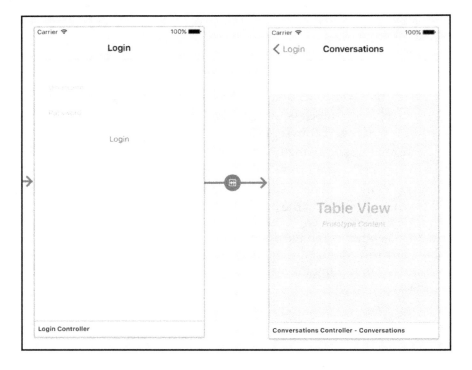

Open `LoginController.cs` and modify the line of code that we marked as `TODO` earlier in this chapter, as follows:

```
PerformSegue("OnLogin", this);
```

Now if you build and run the application, you will navigate to the new controller after a successful login. The segue will be performed, and you will see the built-in animation provided by the navigation controller.

Setting up UITableView

Next, let's set up the table view on the second controller. We are using a powerful class on iOS called `UITableView`. It is used in many situations and is very similar to the concept of a list view on other platforms. The `UITableView` class is controlled by another class called `UITableViewSource`. It has methods that you need to override to set up how many rows should exist and how those rows should be displayed on the screen.

 Note that `UITableViewSource` is a combination of `UITableViewDelegate` and `UITableViewDataSource`. I prefer to use `UITableViewSource` for simplicity, since using both of the other two classes would often be required.

Before we jump in and start coding, let's review the most commonly used methods on `UITableViewSource`, which are as follows:

- `RowsInSection`: This method allows you to define the number of rows in a section. All table views have a number of sections and rows. By default, there is only one section; however, it is a requirement to return the number of rows in a section.
- `NumberOfSections`: This is the number of sections in the table view.
- `GetCell`: This method must return a cell for each row. It is up to the developer to set up what a cell should look like; you can set up the table view to recycle cells. Recycling cells will yield better performance while scrolling.
- `TitleForHeader`: This method, if overridden, is the simplest way to return a string for the title. Each section in a table view can have a standard header view by default.
- `RowSelected`: This method will be called when the user selects a row.

There are additional methods that you can override, but these will get you going in most situations. You can also set up custom headers and footers if you need to develop a custom-styled table view.

Now let's open the `ConversationsController.cs` file and create a nested class inside `ConversationsController`, as follows:

```
class TableSource : UITableViewSource
{
  const string CellName = "ConversationCell";
  readonly MessageViewModel messageViewModel =
    ServiceContainer.Resolve<MessageViewModel>();

  public override nint RowsInSection(
    UITableView tableview, nint section)
  {
    return messageViewModel.Conversations == null ?
      0 : messageViewModel.Conversations.Length;
  }

  public override UITableViewCell GetCell(
    UITableView tableView, NSIndexPath indexPath)
  {
    var conversation =
      messageViewModel.Conversations[indexPath.Row];
    var cell = tableView.DequeueReusableCell(CellName);
    if (cell == null)
    {
      cell = new UITableViewCell(
        UITableViewCellStyle.Default, CellName);
      cell.Accessory =
        UITableViewCellAccessory.DisclosureIndicator;
    }
    cell.TextLabel.Text = conversation.UserName;
    return cell;
  }
}
```

We implemented the two required methods for setting up a table view: `RowsInSection` and `GetCell`. We returned the number of conversations found on the view model and set up our cell for each row. We also used `UITableViewCellAccessory.DisclosureIndicator` to add an indicator for the users to see that they can click on the row.

Notice our implementation of recycling cells. Calling `DequeueReusableCell` with a cell identifier will return a `null` cell the first time around. If `null`, you should create a new cell using the same cell identifier. Subsequent calls to `DequeueReusableCell` will return an existing cell, enabling you to reuse it. You can also define `TableView` cells in the storyboard file, which is useful for custom cells. Our cell here is very simple, so it is easier to define it from the code. Recycling cells is important on mobile platforms to preserve memory and provide the user with a very fluid scrolling table.

Next, we need to set up the `TableView` source on `TableView`. Add some changes to our `ConversationsController` class, as follows:

```
readonly MessageViewModel messageViewModel =
  ServiceContainer.Resolve<MessageViewModel>();

public override void ViewDidLoad()
{
  base.ViewDidLoad();

  TableView.Source = new TableSource();
}

public async override void ViewWillAppear(bool animated)
{
  base.ViewWillAppear(animated);

  try
  {
    await messageViewModel.GetConversations();

    TableView.ReloadData();
  }
  catch(Exception exc)
  {
    new UIAlertView("Oops!", exc.Message, null, "Ok").Show();
  }
}
```

So, when the view appears, we will load our list of conversations. Upon completion of that task, we'll reload the table view so that it displays our list of conversations. If you run the application, you'll see a few conversations appear in the table view after logging in, as shown in the following screenshot. Down the road, everything will operate in the same manner when we load the conversations from a real web service.

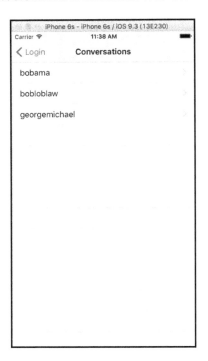

Adding a friends list screen

The next screen we need for our XamSnap app is our friends list. When creating a new conversation, the app will load a list of friends to start a conversation with. We'll follow a very similar pattern to load our list of conversations.

To begin, we'll create `UIBarButtonItem`, which navigates to a new controller named `FriendsController`, by performing the following steps:

1. Double-click on the `Main.storyboard` file to open it in the iOS designer.
2. Add a new **Table View Controller** to the storyboard.

3. Select your view controller, click on the **Properties** pane and make sure you have selected the **Widget** tab.

4. Enter `FriendsController` into the **Class** field.

5. Scroll down to the **View Controller** section and enter `Friends` in the **Title** field.

6. Drag a **Navigation Item** from the **Toolbox** onto the `ConversationsController`.

7. Create a new **Bar Button Item** element and place it on the top-right of the new navigation bar.

8. In the **Properties** pane of the bar button, set its **Identifier** to **Add**. This will use the built-in plus button, which is commonly used throughout iOS applications.

9. Create a segue from the **Bar Button Item** to the `FriendsController` by holding Ctrl and dragging the blue line from the bar button to the next controller.

10. Select the **Show** segue from the pop up that appears.

11. Save the storyboard file.

Your changes to the storyboard should look something similar to what is shown in the following screenshot:

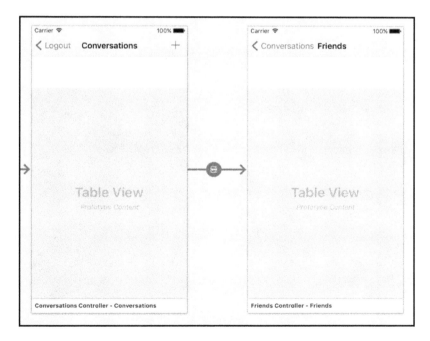

You should see a new `FriendsController` class, which Xamarin Studio has generated for you. If you compile and run the application, you'll see the new bar button item we've created. Clicking on it will navigate you to the new controller.

Now let's implement `UITableViewSource` to display our friends list. Start with a new nested class inside `FriendsController`, as follows:

```
class TableSource : UITableViewSource
{
  const string CellName = "FriendCell";
  readonly FriendViewModel friendViewModel =
    ServiceContainer.Resolve<FriendViewModel>();

  public override nint RowsInSection(
    UITableView tableview, nint section)
  {
    return friendViewModel.Friends == null ?
      0 : friendViewModel.Friends.Length;
  }

  public override UITableViewCell GetCell(
    UITableView tableView, NSIndexPath indexPath)
  {
    var friend =
      friendViewModel.Friends[indexPath.Row];
    var cell = tableView.DequeueReusableCell(CellName);
    if (cell == null)
    {
      cell = new UITableViewCell(
        UITableViewCellStyle.Default, CellName);
      cell.AccessoryView =
        UIButton.FromType(UIButtonType.ContactAdd);
      cell.AccessoryView.UserInteractionEnabled = false;
    }
    cell.TextLabel.Text = friend.Name;
    return cell;
  }
}
```

Just as before, we implemented table cell recycling and merely set the text on the label for each friend. We used `cell.AccessoryView` to indicate to the user that each cell is clickable and starts a new conversation. We disabled user interaction on the button just to allow the row to be selected when the user clicks on the button. Otherwise, we'd have to implement a click event for the button.

Next, we'll need to modify `FriendsController` in the same way as we did for conversations, as follows:

```
readonly FriendViewModel friendViewModel =
   ServiceContainer.Resolve<FriendViewModel>();

public override void ViewDidLoad()
{
  base.ViewDidLoad();

  TableView.Source = new TableSource();
}

public async override void ViewWillAppear(bool animated)
{
  base.ViewWillAppear(animated);

  try
  {
    await friendViewModel.GetFriends();

    TableView.ReloadData();
  }
  catch(Exception exc)
  {
    new UIAlertView("Oops!", exc.Message, null, "Ok").Show();
  }
}
```

This will function exactly the same as the conversations list: the controller will load the friends list asynchronously and refresh the table view. If you compile and run the application, you'll be able to navigate to the screen and view the sample friends list we created in Chapter 4, *XamSnap - A Cross-Platform App*, as shown in the following screenshot:

Adding a list of messages

Now let's implement the screen to view a conversation or list of messages. We will try to model the screen on the built-in text message application in iOS. To do so, we will also cover the basics of how to create custom table view cells.

To start, we'll need a new MessagesController class; perform the following steps:

1. Double-click on the Main.storyboard file to open it in the iOS designer.
2. Add a new **Table View Controller** to the storyboard.
3. Select your view controller, click on the **Properties** pane and make sure you have selected the **Widget** tab.

4. Enter `MessagesController` into the **Class** field.

5. Scroll down to the **View Controller** section and enter `Messages` in the **Title** field.

6. Create a segue from `ConversationsController` to `MessagesController` by holding *Ctrl* and dragging the blue line from one controller to the other.

7. Select the **Show** segue from the pop up that appears. Enter the **Identifier** `OnConversation` in the **Properties** pane.

8. Now create two **Table View Cells** in the table view in `MessagesController`. You may reuse the existing blank one created by default.

9. Change the **Style** field to **Basic** for each cell.

10. Set the **Identifier** to `MyCell` and `TheirCell`, respectively, for each cell.

11. Save the storyboard file.

Xamarin Studio will generate `MessagesController.cs`. Just as before, you can move the controller to a `Controllers` folder. Now open `MessagesController.cs` and implement `UITableViewSource` inside a nested class, as follows:

```
class TableSource : UITableViewSource
{
  const string MyCellName = "MyCell";
  const string TheirCellName = "TheirCell";
  readonly MessageViewModel messageViewModel =
    ServiceContainer.Resolve();
  readonly ISettings settings = ServiceContainer.Resolve();

  public override nint RowsInSection(
    UITableView tableview, nint section)
  {
    return messageViewModel.Messages == null ? 0 :
      messageViewModel.Messages.Length;
  }

  public override UITableViewCell GetCell(
    UITableView tableView, NSIndexPath indexPath)
  {
    var message = messageViewModel.Messages [indexPath.Row];
    bool isMyMessage = message.UserName == settings.User.Name;
    var cell = (BaseMessageCell)tableView.DequeueReusableCell(
      isMyMessage ? MyCellName : TheirCellName);
    cell.TextLabel.Text = message.Text;
    return cell;
  }
}
```

We added some logic to check if a message is from a current user to decide on the appropriate table cell identifier. Since we used the **Basic** style for both cells, we can use the `TextLabel` property on the cell to set the text for a `UILabel`.

Now let's make the required changes to our `MessagesController`, as follows:

```
readonly MessageViewModel messageViewModel =
  ServiceContainer.Resolve<MessageViewModel>();

public override void ViewDidLoad()
{
  base.ViewDidLoad();

  TableView.Source = new TableSource();
}

public async override void ViewWillAppear(bool animated)
{
  base.ViewWillAppear(animated);

  Title = messageViewModel.Conversation.UserName;
  try
  {
    await messageViewModel.GetMessages();
    TableView.ReloadData();
  }
  catch (Exception exc)
  {
    new UIAlertView("Oops!", exc.Message, null, "Ok").Show();
  }
}
```

The only new thing here is where we set the `Title` property to the username of the conversation.

To complete our custom cells, we will need to make more changes in Xcode by performing the following steps:

1. Double-click on the `Main.storyboard` file to open it in the iOS designer.
2. Select a **Label** by clicking on the default text, **Title**, on either cell.
3. Use some creativity to style both labels. I chose to make the text in `MyCell` blue and `TheirCell` green. I set **Alignment** on the label to right aligned in `TheirCell`.
4. Save the storyboard file and return.

Next, we need to update the `ConversationsController` to navigate to this new screen. Let's modify the `TableSource` class inside `ConversationsController.cs`, as follows:

```
readonly ConversationsController controller;

public TableSource(ConversationsController controller)
{
  this.controller = controller;
}

public override void RowSelected(
  UITableView tableView, NSIndexPath indexPath)
{
  var conversation = messageViewModel.Conversations[indexPath.Row];
  messageViewModel.Conversation = conversation;
  controller.PerformSegue("OnConversation", this);
}
```

And, of course, you will have to modify one small line in the `ViewDidLoad` of the controller:

```
TableView.Source = new TableSource(this);
```

If you run the application now, you will be able to view the messages list as displayed in the following screenshot:

Composing messages

For the final piece of our application, we need to implement some custom functionality that Apple doesn't provide with their APIs. We need to add a text field with a button that appears to be attached to the bottom of the table view. Most of this will require writing some simple C# code and wiring up events.

Let's begin by adding some new member variables to our `MessagesController` class, as follows:

```
UIToolbar toolbar;
UITextField message;
UIBarButtonItem send;
```

We will place the text field and bar buttons inside the toolbar, as in the following code in `ViewDidLoad`:

```
public override void ViewDidLoad()
{
  base.ViewDidLoad();

  //Text Field
  message = new UITextField(
    new CGRect(0, 0, TableView.Frame.Width - 88, 32))
  {
    BorderStyle = UITextBorderStyle.RoundedRect,
    ReturnKeyType = UIReturnKeyType.Send,
    ShouldReturn = _ =>
    {
        Send();
        return false;
    },
  };

  //Bar button item
  send = new UIBarButtonItem("Send", UIBarButtonItemStyle.Plain,
    (sender, e) => Send());

  //Toolbar
  toolbar = new UIToolbar(
    new CGRect(0, TableView.Frame.Height - 44,
      TableView.Frame.Width, 44));
  toolbar.Items = new[]
  {
    new UIBarButtonItem(message),
    send
  };
```

```
    TableView.Source = new TableSource();
    TableView.TableFooterView = toolbar;
}
```

Much of this work is a basic UI setup. It is not something we can do inside Xcode because it is a very specific use case. We create a text field, bar button item, and toolbar from C#, and add them as a footer to our `UITableView`. This will display the toolbar at the bottom of the table view, below any rows we defined earlier.

Now we will need to modify `ViewWillAppear`, as follows:

```
public async override void ViewWillAppear(bool animated)
{
    base.ViewWillAppear(animated);

    Title = messageViewModel.Conversation.Username;

    messageViewModel.IsBusyChanged += OnIsBusyChanged;

    try
    {
        await messageViewModel.GetMessages();
        TableView.ReloadData();
        message.BecomeFirstResponder();
    }
    catch (Exception exc)
    {
        new UIAlertView("Oops!", exc.Message, null, "Ok").Show();
    }
}
```

We need to subscribe to `IsBusyChanged` in order to show and hide the spinner. We also call `BecomeFirstResponder`, so the keyboard will appear and give focus to our text field.

So let's add an override for `ViewWillDisapper` to clean up the event, as follows:

```
public override void ViewWillDisappear(bool animated)
{
    base.ViewWillDisappear(animated);
    messageViewModel.IsBusyChanged -= OnIsBusyChanged;
}
```

Next, let's set up our method for `IsBusyChanged`, as follows:

```
void OnIsBusyChanged (object sender, EventArgs e)
{
  message.Enabled = send.Enabled = !messageViewModel.IsBusy;
}
```

`OnIsBusyChanged` is used to disable some of our views while it is loading.

Last but not least, we need to implement a function for sending a new message, as follows:

```
async void Send()
{
  //Just hide the keyboard if they didn't type anything
  if (string.IsNullOrEmpty(message.Text))
  {
    message.ResignFirstResponder();
    return;
  }

  //Set the text, send the message
  messageViewModel.Text = message.Text;
  await messageViewModel.SendMessage();

  //Clear the text field & view model
  message.Text = messageViewModel.Text = string.Empty;

  //Reload the table
  TableView.InsertRows(new[]
  {
    NSIndexPath.FromRowSection(
      messageViewModel.Messages.Length - 1, 0)
  }, UITableViewRowAnimation.Automatic);
}
```

This code is also fairly straightforward. After sending the message, we merely need to clear out the text field and tell the table view to reload the newly added row, as shown in the following screenshot. Using the `async` keyword makes this easy.

Summary

In this chapter, we covered the basic settings that Apple and Xamarin provide for developing iOS applications. This includes the `Info.plist` file and project options in Xamarin Studio. We covered `UINavigationController`, the basic building block for navigation in iOS applications, and implemented a login screen complete with username and password fields. Next, we covered iOS segues and the `UITableView` class. We implemented the friends list screen using `UITableView`, and the messages list screen, also using `UITableView`. Lastly, we added a custom UI functionality: a custom toolbar floating at the bottom of the messages list.

Upon completing this chapter, you will have a partially functional iOS version of XamSnap. You will have a deeper understanding of the iOS platform and tools, and fairly good knowledge to apply to building your own iOS applications. Take it upon yourself to implement the remaining screens that we did not cover in this chapter. If you get lost, feel free to review the full sample application included with this book.

In the next chapter, we will implement these UIs on Android.

6
XamSnap for Android

To begin writing the Android version of XamSnap, open the solution from the previous two chapters. We'll be working in the `XamSnap.Droid` project, which should be already setup from the Xamarin project template.

In this chapter, we will cover:

- The Android manifest
- Android Material Design
- Writing a login screen for XamSnap
- Android's ListView and BaseAdapter
- Adding a friends list
- Adding a list of messages

Introducing the Android Manifest

All Android applications have an XML file called the Android Manifest, which declares basic information about the app, and is named `AndroidManifest.xml`. This is very similar to the `Info.plist` file on iOS, except Xamarin also provides C# class attributes for placing common settings in the Android manifest. There is also a nice UI for editing the manifest under **Project Options | Android Application**.

The most important settings, shown in the following screenshot, are as follows:

- **Application name**: This is the title of your application, which is displayed below the icon. It is not the same as the name selected on Google Play.
- **Package name**: This is just like on iOS, your app's bundle identifier. It is a unique name to identify your application. The convention is to use the reverse domain style with your company name at the beginning; for example, `com.jonathanpeppers.xamsnap`. It must begin with a lower case letter and contain at least one character within.
- **Application icon**: This is the icon displayed for your app on Android's home screen.
- **Version number**: This is a one-digit number that represents the version of your application. Raising this number indicates a newer version on Google Play.
- **Version name**: This is a user-friendly version string for your app; for example, **1.0.0**.
- **Minimum Android version**: This is the minimum version of Android that your application supports.
- **Target Android version**: This is the version of the Android SDK your application is compiled against. Using higher numbers gives you access to new APIs; however, you might need to do some runtime checks to not call these APIs on older devices.
- **Install Location**: This defines the different locations that your Android application can be installed to: auto (user settings), external (SD card), or internal (device internal memory).

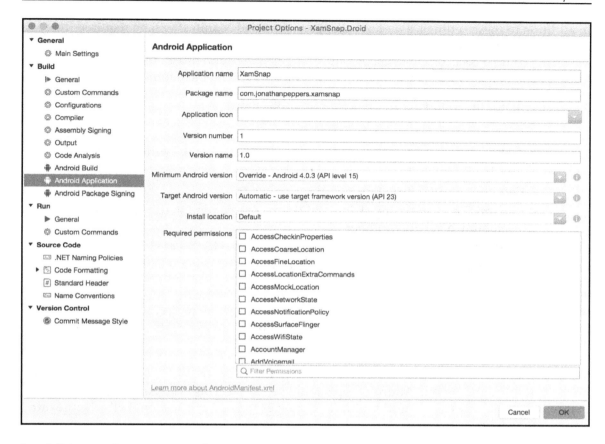

In addition to these settings, there is a set of checkboxes labeled **Required permissions**. These are displayed to users on Google Play prior to the application being installed. This is Android's way of enforcing a level of security, giving users a way to see what kinds of access an app will have to make changes to their device.

The following are some commonly used manifest permissions:

- **Camera**: This provides access to the device camera
- **Internet**: This provides access to make web requests over the Internet
- **ReadContacts**: This provides access to read the device's contacts library
- **ReadExternalStorage**: This provides access to read the SD card
- **WriteContacts**: This provides access to modify the device's contacts library
- **WriteExternalStorage**: This provides access to write to the SD card

In addition to these settings, a manual change to Android Manifest will be required many times. In this case, you can edit the manifest file as you would a standard XML file in Xamarin Studio. For a complete list of valid XML elements and attributes, visit http://developer.android.com/guide/topics/manifest/manifest-intro.html.

Now let's fill out the following settings for our application:

- **Application name**: XamSnap
- **Package name**: com.yourcompanyname.xamsnap; make sure to name future apps beginning with com.yourcompanyname
- **Version number**: Just start with the number 1
- **Version**: This can be any string, but it is recommended to use something resembling a version number
- **Minimum Android version**: Select **Android 4.0.3 (API Level 15)**
- **Required permissions**: Select **Internet**; we will be using it later

At this point, notice that our Android project is already referencing our shared code from our portable class library. Expand the **References** folder for the project and notice the reference to the XamSnap.Core project. We will be able to access all the shared code that was written in Chapter 4, *XamSnap – A Cross-Platform App*.

Go to the Resources directory, and in the values folder open Strings.xml; this is where all the text throughout your Android app should be stored. This is an Android convention that will make it very easy to add multiple languages to your application. Let's change our strings to the following:

```
<?xml version="1.0" encoding="utf-8"?>
<resources>
    <string name="ApplicationName">XamSnap</string>
    <string name="ErrorTitle">Oops!</string>
    <string name="Loading">Loading</string>
    <string name="Login">Login</string>
</resources>
```

We'll use these values later in the chapter; feel free to add new ones in cases where you display text to the user.

Setting up Material Design

Beginning with Android 5.0 Lollipop, Google released a new theme and color palette for Android applications called **Material Design**. It is a good idea to adopt material design for new apps, as it gives you a modern Android look, with little effort to setup. For more information on material design, check out Google's documentation at: https://developer.android.com/design/material/index.html.

To make material design (and other new Android features) easier to adopt, Google has also released an **AppCompat** library for Android so you can support these newer features on older Android OS versions. Xamarin supports a version of the AppCompat library on NuGet so that it is easy to set up for Xamarin.Android applications.

To set up the Android support library, follow these steps:

1. Right-click on **Packages** and select **Add Packages**.
2. Search for `Xamarin.Android.Support.v7.AppCompat`.
3. Click **Add Package**.
4. NuGet will download the library and its dependencies, referencing them in your Android project.

Now let's implement our main application class; add a new **Activity** from the **New File** dialog. We won't be subclassing `Activity` in this file, but this template adds several Android `using` statements to the top of the file that imports the Android APIs to be used within your code. Create a new `Application` class where we can register everything in our `ServiceContainer` as follows:

```
[Application(Theme = "@style/Theme.AppCompat.Light")]
public class Application : Android.App.Application
{
  public Application(
     IntPtr javaReference, JniHandleOwnership transfer)
     : base(javaReference, transfer)
  {
  }

  public override void OnCreate()
  {
    base.OnCreate();

    //ViewModels
    ServiceContainer.Register<LoginViewModel>(
       () => new LoginViewModel());
    ServiceContainer.Register<FriendViewModel>(
```

```
        () => new FriendViewModel());
    ServiceContainer.Register<MessageViewModel>(
        () => new MessageViewModel());
    ServiceContainer.Register<RegisterViewModel>(
        () => new RegisterViewModel());

    //Models
    ServiceContainer.Register<ISettings>(
        () => new FakeSettings());
    ServiceContainer.Register<IWebService>(
        () => new FakeWebService());
    }
  }
```

We used the built-in Android theme, `Theme.AppCompat.Light`, it is the default light theme for material design. Note the strange constructor we have to follow, this is a current requirement of a custom `Application` class in Xamarin. You can just recognize this as boilerplate code that you will need to add this in this case.

Now let's implement a simple base class for all the activities throughout our app. Create an `Activities` folder in the `XamSnap.Droid` project and a new file named `BaseActivity.cs` with the following contents:

```
[Activity]
public class BaseActivity<TViewModel> : AppCompatActivity
   where TViewModel : BaseViewModel
{
  protected readonly TViewModel viewModel;
  protected ProgressDialog progress;

  public BaseActivity()
  {
    viewModel = ServiceContainer.Resolve(typeof(TViewModel)) as
      TViewModel;
  }
  protected override void OnCreate(Bundle savedInstanceState)
  {
    base.OnCreate(savedInstanceState);

    progress = new ProgressDialog(this);
    progress.SetCancelable(false);
    progress.SetTitle(Resource.String.Loading);
  }

  protected override void OnResume()
  {
    base.OnResume();
```

[124]

```
    viewModel.IsBusyChanged += OnIsBusyChanged;
  }

  protected override void OnPause()
  {
    base.OnPause();
    viewModel.IsBusyChanged -= OnIsBusyChanged;
  }

  void OnIsBusyChanged (object sender, EventArgs e)
  {
    if (viewModel.IsBusy)
      progress.Show();
    else
      progress.Hide();
  }
}
```

We did several things here to simplify the development of our other activities. First, we made this class generic, and made a protected variable named viewModel to store a view model of a specific type. Note that we did not use generics on controllers in iOS due to platform limitations (see more on Xamarin's documentation website at http://developer. xamarin.com/guides/ios/advanced_topics/limitations/). We also implemented IsBusyChanged, and displayed a simple ProgressDialog with the Loading string from the Strings.xml file to indicate network activity.

Let's add one more method for displaying errors to the user as follows:

```
  protected void DisplayError(Exception exc)
  {
    string error = exc.Message;
    new AlertDialog.Builder(this)
      .SetTitle(Resource.String.ErrorTitle)
      .SetMessage(error)
      .SetPositiveButton(Android.Resource.String.Ok,
        (IDialogInterfaceOnClickListener)null)
      .Show();
  }
```

This method will display a pop-up dialog, indicating that something went wrong. Notice we also used ErrorTitle and the built-in Android resource for an Ok string.

This will complete the core setup for our Android application. From here we can move on to implement the UI for the screens throughout our app.

Adding a login screen

Before creating Android views, it is important to know the different layouts or view group types available in Android. iOS does not have an equivalent for some of these because iOS has a smaller variation of screen sizes on its devices. Since Android has virtually infinite screen sizes and densities, the Android SDK has a lot of built-in support for auto-sizing and layout for views.

The following are the common types of layouts:

- `ViewGroup`: This is the base class for a view that contains a collection of child views. You normally won't use this class directly.
- `LinearLayout`: This is a layout that positions its child views in rows or columns (but not both). You can also set weights on each child, to have them span different percentages of the available space.
- `RelativeLayout`: This is a layout that gives much more flexibility on the position of its children. You can position child views relative to each other so that they are above, below, to the left, or to the right of one another.
- `FrameLayout`: This layout positions its child views directly on top of one another in the **z order** on the screen. This layout is best used for cases where you have a large child view that needs other views on top of it and perhaps docked to one side.
- `ListView`: This displays views vertically in a list with the help of an adapter class that determines the number of child views. It also has support for its children to be selected.
- `GridView`: This displays views in rows and columns within a grid. It also requires the use of an adapter class to supply the number of children.

Before we begin writing the login screen, delete the `Main.axml` and `MainActivity.cs` files that were created from the Android project template. Next, create an Android layout file named `Login.axml` in the `layout` folder of the `Resources` directory in your project.

Now we can start adding functionalities to our Android layout as follows:

1. Double-click on the new layout file to open the Android designer.
2. Drag two **Plain Text** views onto the layout found in the **Text Fields** section.
3. In the **Id** field, enter `@+id/username` and `@+id/password`, respectively.
4. For the password field, set its **Input Type** property to `textPassword`.
5. Drag a **Button** onto the layout and set its **Text** property to `@string/Login`.
6. Set the button's **Id** property to `@+id/login`.

Your layout will look something like the following screenshot when complete:

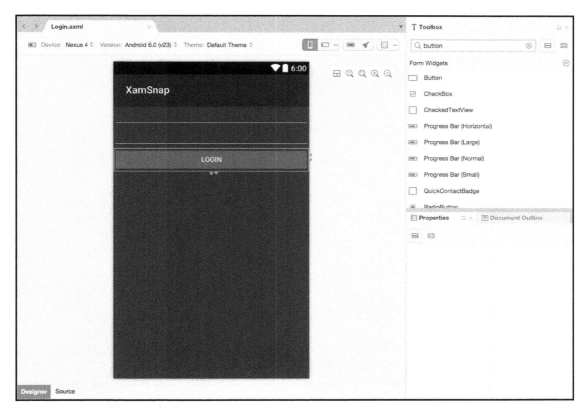

Now create a new Android Activity file named `LoginActivity.cs` in the `Activites` folder we created earlier. Let's implement the login functionality as follows:

```
[Activity(Label = "@string/ApplicationName", MainLauncher = true)]
public class LoginActivity : BaseActivity<LoginViewModel>
{
  EditText username, password;
  Button login;

  protected override void OnCreate(Bundle savedInstanceState)
  {
    base.OnCreate(savedInstanceState);

    SetContentView(Resource.Layout.Login);
    username = FindViewById<EditText>(Resource.Id.username);
    password = FindViewById<EditText>(Resource.Id.password);
    login = FindViewById<Button>(Resource.Id.login);
```

```
      login.Click += OnLogin;
  }

  protected override void OnResume()
  {
    base.OnResume();
    username.Text =
       password.Text = string.Empty;
  }

  async void OnLogin (object sender, EventArgs e)
  {
    viewModel.UserName = username.Text;
    viewModel.Password = password.Text;
    try
    {
      await viewModel.Login();
      //TODO: navigate to a new activity
    }
    catch (Exception exc)
    {
      DisplayError(exc);
    }
  }
}
```

Notice that we set `MainLauncher` to `true`, to make this activity the first activity for the application. We also took advantage of the `ApplicationName` value and `BaseActivity` class we set up earlier in this chapter. We also overrode `OnResume` to clear out the two `EditText` controls so that the values are cleared out if you return to the screen.

Now if you launch the application, you will be greeted by the login screen we just implemented, as shown in the following screenshot:

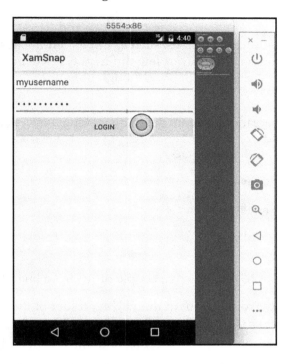

Just a note for Visual Studio users, Xamarin has done a great job making their Visual Studio Extension work identical to Xamarin Studio. All of the examples in this chapter should work just as described in either Xamarin Studio on OS X or Visual Studio on Windows.

Using ListView and BaseAdapter

Now let's implement a conversations list on Android. The Android equivalent of UITableView and UITableViewSource are ListView and BaseAdapter. There are parallel concepts for these Android classes, such as implementing abstract methods and recycling cells during scrolling. There are a few different types of adapters used in Android such as ArrayAdapter or CursorAdaptor, although BaseAdapter is generally best suited for simple lists.

Let's implement our conversations screen. Begin by making a new Android Activity in your Activities folder named ConversationsActivity.cs. Let's start with only a couple of changes to the class definition, as follows:

```
[Activity(Label = "Conversations")]
public class ConversationsActivity :
   BaseActivity<MessageViewModel>
{
  //Other code here later
}
```

Perform the following steps to implement a couple of Android layouts:

1. Create a new Android Layout in the layout folder of the Resources directory named Conversations.axml.
2. Drag a **ListView** control from **Toolbox** onto the layout and set its **Id** to @+id/conversationsList.
3. Create a second Android Layout; the layout folder in the Resources directory named ConversationListItem.axml.
4. Drag a **Text (Medium)** control onto the layout from the **Toolbox**.
5. Set its ID to @+id/conversationUsername.
6. Finally, let's set its **Margin** to 3dp in the **Layout** tab of the **Properties** box.

This will set up all the layout files that we'll need to use throughout the conversations screen. Your ConversationListItem.axml layout will look something like what's shown in the following screenshot:

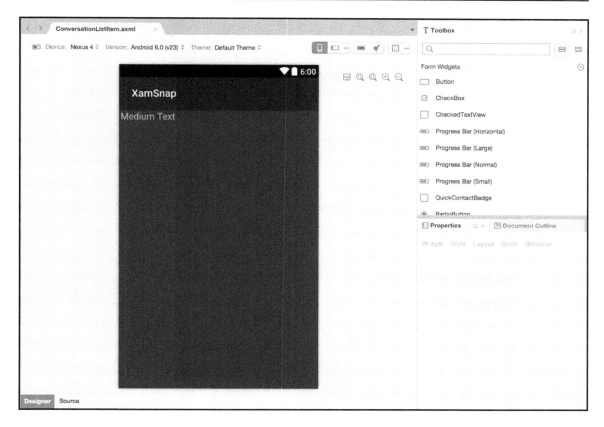

Now we can implement `BaseAdapter` as a nested class inside of `ConversationsActivity`, as follows:

```
class Adapter : BaseAdapter<Conversation>
{
  readonly MessageViewModel messageViewModel =
    ServiceContainer.Resolve<MessageViewModel>();
  readonly LayoutInflater inflater;

  public Adapter(Context context)
  {
    inflater = (LayoutInflater)context.GetSystemService(
      Context.LayoutInflaterService);
  }

  public override long GetItemId(int position)
  {
    //This is an abstract method, just a simple implementation
```

```
      return position;
    }

    public override View GetView(
        int position, View convertView, ViewGroup parent)
    {
      if (convertView == null)
      {
        convertView = inflater.Inflate(
          Resource.Layout.ConversationListItem, null);
      }
      var conversation = this [position];
      var username = convertView.FindViewById<TextView>(
        Resource.Id.conversationUsername);
      username.Text = conversation.Username;
      return convertView;
    }

    public override int Count
    {
      get { return messageViewModel.Conversations == null ? 0
        : messageViewModel.Conversations.Length; }
    }

    public override Conversation this[int position]
    {
      get { return messageViewModel.Conversations [position]; }
    }
  }
```

The following is a review of what is going on inside the adapter:

- We subclassed `BaseAdapter<Conversation>`.
- We passed in a `Context` (our activity) so that we can pull out the `LayoutInflater`. This class enables us to load XML layout resources and inflate them into a view object.
- We implemented `GetItemId`. This is a general method used to identify rows, but we just returned the position for now.
- We set up `GetView`, which recycles the `convertView` variable by only creating a new view if it is null. We also pulled out the text views in our layout to set their text.
- We overrode `Count` to return the number of conversations.
- We implemented an indexer to return a `Conversation` object for a position.

Overall, this should be fairly similar to what we did on iOS.

Now let's set up the adapter in our activity by adding the following to the body of
`ConversationsActivity`:

```
ListView listView;
Adapter adapter;

protected override void OnCreate(Bundle bundle)
{
  base.OnCreate(bundle);

  SetContentView(Resource.Layout.Conversations);
  listView = FindViewById<ListView>(
     Resource.Id.conversationsList);
  listView.Adapter =
     adapter = new Adapter(this);
}

protected async override void OnResume()
{
  base.OnResume();
  try
  {
    await viewModel.GetConversations();
    adapter.NotifyDataSetInvalidated();
  }
  catch (Exception exc)
  {
    DisplayError(exc);
  }
}
```

This code will set up the adapter and reload our list of conversations when the activity
appears on screen. Note that we called `NotifyDataSetInvalidated` here, so that
`ListView` reloads its rows after the number of conversations has been updated.

Last but not least, we need to modify the `OnLogin` method we set up earlier in
`LoginActivity` to start our new activity as follows:

```
StartActivity(typeof(ConversationsActivity));
```

Now if we compile and run our application, we can navigate to a conversations list after logging in, as shown in the following screenshot:

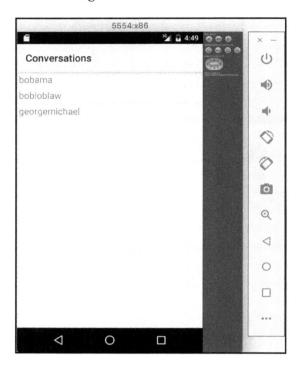

Implementing the friends list

Before we start implementing the friends list screen, we must first add a menu item to `ActionBar` in our application. Begin by creating a new `menu` folder within the `Resources` folder of our project. Next, create a new Android Layout file named `ConversationsMenu.axml`. Remove the default layout XML created, and replace it with the following:

```
<?xml version="1.0" encoding="utf-8"?>
<menu xmlns:android="http://schemas.android.com/apk/res/android">
  <item android:id="@+id/addFriendMenu"
     android:text="Add Friend"
     android:showAsAction="ifRoom"/>
</menu>
```

We set up a root menu with one menu item inside it.

The following is a breakdown of what we set for the item in XML:

- `android:id`: We will use this later in C# to reference the menu item with `Resource.Id.addFriendMenu`.
- `android:icon`: This is an image resource to display for the menu item. We used a built-in Android one for a generic *plus* icon.
- `android:showAsAction`: This will make the menu item visible if there is room. If for some reason the device's screen is too narrow, an overflow menu would be displayed for the menu item.

Now we can make some changes in `ConversationsActivity.cs` to display the menu item as follows:

```
public override bool OnCreateOptionsMenu(IMenu menu)
{
  MenuInflater.Inflate(Resource.Menu.ConversationsMenu, menu);
  return base.OnCreateOptionsMenu(menu);
}
```

This code will take our layout and apply it to the menu at the top in our activity's action bar. Next, we can add some code to be run when the menu item is selected, as follows:

```
public override bool OnOptionsItemSelected(IMenuItem item)
{
  if (item.ItemId == Resource.Id.addFriendMenu)
  {
    //TODO: launch the next activity
  }
  return base.OnOptionsItemSelected(item);
}
```

Now let's implement the next activity. Begin by making a copy of `Conversations.axml`, found in the `layout` folder in the `Resources` directory, and rename it to `Friends.axml`. The only change we'll make in this file will be to rename the ListView's ID to `@+id/friendsList`.

Next, perform the following steps to create a layout that can be used for the list items in `ListView`:

1. Make a new Android Layout called `FriendListItem.axml`.
2. Open the layout and switch to the **Source** tab found at the bottom of the screen.
3. Change the root `LinearLayout` XML element to a `RelativeLayout` element.
4. Switch back to the **Designer** tab found at the bottom of the screen.

5. Drag a **Text (Large)** control from the **Toolbox** onto the layout and set its **Id** to `@+id/friendName`.

6. Drag an **ImageView** control from the **Toolbox** onto the layout; you can either let its **Id** be its default value or blank it out.

7. Change the image view's image to `@android:drawable/ic_menu_add`. This is the same plus icon we used earlier in this chapter. You can select it from the **Resources** dialog under the **Framework Resources** tab.

8. Set the **Width** and **Height** of both the controls to `wrap_content`. This is found under the **Layout** tab, under the **ViewGroup** section.

9. Next, check the value for **Align Parent Right** on just the image view.

10. Finally, set the **Margins** of both the controls to `3dp` in the **Layout** tab of the **Properties** box.

Using the Xamarin designer can be very productive, but some developers prefer a higher level of control. You might consider writing the XML yourself as an alternative, which is fairly straightforward, as in the following code:

```xml
<?xml version="1.0" encoding="utf-8"?>
<RelativeLayout
    xmlns:android="http://schemas.android.com/apk/res/android"
    android:layout_width="fill_parent"
    android:layout_height="fill_parent">
    <TextView
        android:text="Large Text"
        android:textAppearance="?android:attr/textAppearanceLarge"
        android:layout_width="wrap_content"
        android:layout_height="wrap_content"
        android:id="@+id/friendName"
        android:layout_margin="3dp" />
    <ImageView
        android:layout_width="wrap_content"
        android:layout_height="wrap_content"
        android:src="@android:drawable/ic_menu_add"
        android:layout_margin="3dp"
        android:layout_alignParentRight="true" />
</RelativeLayout>
```

Since we now have all the layouts we need for the new screen, let's create an Android Activity in the `Activities` folder named `FriendsActivity.cs`. Let's create the basic definition of the activity as follows, just like we did before:

```
[Activity(Label = "Friends")]
public class FriendsActivity : BaseActivity<FriendViewModel>
```

```
{
  protected override void OnCreate(Bundle savedInstanceState)
  {
    base.OnCreate(savedInstanceState);
  }
}
```

Now, let's implement a nested `Adapter` class for setting up the list view items, as follows:

```
class Adapter : BaseAdapter<User>
{
  readonly FriendViewModel friendViewModel =
     ServiceContainer.Resolve<FriendViewModel>();
  readonly LayoutInflater inflater;

  public Adapter(Context context)
  {
    inflater = (LayoutInflater)context.GetSystemService (
       Context.LayoutInflaterService);
  }

  public override long GetItemId(int position)
  {
    return position;
  }

  public override View GetView(
     int position, View convertView, ViewGroup parent)
  {
    if (convertView == null)
    {
      convertView = inflater.Inflate(
         Resource.Layout.FriendListItem, null);
    }
    var friend = this [position];
    var friendname = convertView.FindViewById<TextView>(
       Resource.Id.friendName);
    friendname.Text = friend.Name;
    return convertView;
  }

  public override int Count
  {
    get { return friendViewModel.Friends == null ? 0
       : friendViewModel.Friends.Length; }
  }

  public override User this[int position]
```

```
    {
      get { return friendViewModel.Friends[position]; }
    }
  }
```

There is really no difference in this adapter and the previous one we implemented for the conversations screen. We only have to set the friend's name, and we use the `User` object instead of the `Conversation` object.

To finish setting up the adapter, we can update the body of the `FriendsActivity` class, as follows:

```
ListView listView;
Adapter adapter;

protected override void OnCreate(Bundle savedInstanceState)
{
  base.OnCreate(savedInstanceState);

  SetContentView(Resource.Layout.Friends);
  listView = FindViewById<ListView>(Resource.Id.friendsList);
  listView.Adapter =
      adapter = new Adapter(this);
}

protected async override void OnResume()
{
  base.OnResume();
  try
  {
    await viewModel.GetFriends();
    adapter.NotifyDataSetInvalidated();
  }
  catch (Exception exc)
  {
    DisplayError(exc);
  }
}
```

And last but not least, we can update `OnOptionsItemSelected` in the `ConversationsActivity` class, as follows:

```
public override bool OnOptionsItemSelected(IMenuItem item)
{
  if (item.ItemId == Resource.Id.addFriendMenu)
  {
    StartActivity(typeof(FriendsActivity));
```

```
        }
        return base.OnOptionsItemSelected(item);
    }
```

So if we compile and run the application, we can navigate to a fully implemented friends list screen, as shown in the following screenshot:

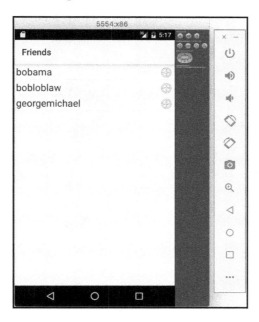

Composing messages

The next screen is a bit more complicated; we will need to create a `ListView` that uses multiple layout files for each row, depending on the type of the row. We'll also need to perform some layout tricks to place a view below the `ListView` and set up the `ListView` to autoscroll.

For the next screen, let's begin by creating a new layout named `Messages.axml` in the `layout` folder of the `Resources` directory and then perform the following steps:

1. Drag a new **ListView** onto the layout. Set its **Id** to `@+id/messageList`.
2. Check the box for **Stack From Bottom**, and set **Transcript Mode** to `alwaysScroll`. This will set it up to display items from the bottom up.
3. Set the **Weight** value to 1 for the **ListView** in the **Layout** tab under the

       LinearLayout section.

4. Drag a new **RelativeLayout** onto the layout. Let its **Id** be the default value, or remove it.

5. Drag a new **Button** inside **RelativeLayout**. Set its **Id** to `@+id/sendButton`.

6. Check the box for **Align Parent Right** in the **Layout** tab.

7. Drag a new **Plain Text** found in the **Text Field** section inside **RelativeLayout** to the left of the button. Set its **Id** to `@+id/messageText`.

8. In the **Layout** tab, set **To Left Of** to `@+id/sendButton`, and set its **Width** to `match_parent`.

9. Check the box for **Center in Parent** to fix the vertical centering.

When completed, the XML file will be as follows:

```xml
<?xml version="1.0" encoding="utf-8"?>
<LinearLayout
    xmlns:android="http://schemas.android.com/apk/res/android"
    android:orientation="vertical"
    android:layout_width="match_parent"
    android:layout_height="match_parent">
    <ListView
        android:minWidth="25px"
        android:minHeight="25px"
        android:layout_width="match_parent"
        android:layout_height="match_parent"
        android:id="@+id/messageList"
        android:stackFromBottom="true"
        android:transcriptMode="alwaysScroll"
        android:layout_weight="1" />
    <RelativeLayout
        android:minWidth="25px"
        android:minHeight="25px"
        android:layout_width="match_parent"
        android:layout_height="wrap_content">
        <EditText
            android:layout_width="match_parent"
            android:layout_height="wrap_content"
            android:id="@+id/messageText"
            android:layout_toLeftOf="@+id/sendButton"
            android:layout_centerInParent="true" />
        <Button
            android:text="Send"
            android:layout_width="wrap_content"
            android:layout_height="wrap_content"
            android:id="@+id/sendButton"
            android:layout_alignParentRight="true" />
```

```
    </RelativeLayout>
  </LinearLayout>
```

Next, perform the following steps to make two more Android layouts:

1. Create a new layout named `MyMessageListItem.axml` in the `layout` folder of the `Resources` directory.
2. Open the layout and switch to the **Source** tab. Change the root XML element to a `RelativeLayout`.
3. Switch back to the **Content** tab and drag two **TextView** controls onto the layout.
4. In the **Id** field, enter `@+id/myMessageText` and `@+id/myMessageDate`, respectively.
5. For both the views, set **Margin** to `3dp`, and **Width** and **Height** to `wrap_content`.
6. For the first TextView, set its **Color** under the **Style** tab to `@android:color/holo_blue_bright`.
7. For the second TextView, check the **Align Parent Right** checkbox under the **Layout** tab.
8. Create a new layout named `TheirMessageListItem.axml` and repeat the process. Select a different color for the first TextView in the new layout.

Finally, we'll need to create a new activity for the screen. Create a new Android Activity named `MessagesActivity.cs` in the `Activities` directory. Begin with the standard code to set up an activity, as follows:

```
[Activity(Label = "Messages")]
public class MessagesActivity : BaseActivity<MessageViewModel>
{
  protected override void OnCreate(Bundle savedInstanceState)
  {
    base.OnCreate(savedInstanceState);
  }
}
```

Next, let's implement a more complicated adapter than what we implemented earlier, as follows:

```
class Adapter : BaseAdapter<Message>
{
  readonly MessageViewModel messageViewModel =
    ServiceContainer.Resolve<MessageViewModel>();
  readonly ISettings settings =
    ServiceContainer.Resolve<ISettings>();
  readonly LayoutInflater inflater;
  const int MyMessageType = 0, TheirMessageType = 1;
```

```
public Adapter (Context context)
{
  inflater = (LayoutInflater)context.GetSystemService (
    Context.LayoutInflaterService);
}

public override long GetItemId(int position)
{
  return position;
}

public override int Count
{
  get { return messageViewModel.Messages == null ? 0
    : messageViewModel.Messages.Length; }
}

public override Message this[int position]
{
  get { return messageViewModel.Messages[position]; }
}

public override int ViewTypeCount
{
  get { return 2; }
}

public override int GetItemViewType(int position)
{
  var message = this [position];
  return message.UserName == settings.User.Name ?
    MyMessageType : TheirMessageType;
}
}
```

This includes everything except our implementation of GetView, which we'll get to shortly. The first changes here are some constants for MyMessageType and TheirMessageType. We then implemented ViewTypeCount and GetItemViewType. This is Android's mechanism for using two different layouts for list items in a list view. We use one type of layout for the user's messages and a different one for the other user in the conversation.

Next, let's implement `GetView` as follows:

```
public override View GetView(
    int position, View convertView, ViewGroup parent)
{
  var message = this [position];
  int type = GetItemViewType(position);
  if (convertView == null)
  {
    if (type == MyMessageType)
    {
      convertView = inflater.Inflate(
        Resource.Layout.MyMessageListItem, null);
    }
    else
    {
      convertView = inflater.Inflate(
        Resource.Layout.TheirMessageListItem, null);
    }
  }
  TextView messageText;
  if (type == MyMessageType)
  {
    messageText = convertView.FindViewById<TextView>(
      Resource.Id.myMessageText);
  }
  else
  {
    messageText = convertView.FindViewById<TextView>(
      Resource.Id.theirMessageText);
  }
  messageText.Text = message.Text;
  return convertView;
}
```

Just a note, it is best practice in Android to use unique ID for each view. It is best even in this case where the code gets a bit ugly, but `FindViewById` does not work as intended when multiple layouts exist with views containing the same ID.

Let's break down our implementation through the following steps:

1. We first pull out the `message` object for the position of the row.
2. Next, we grab the view type that determines if it is the current user's message or the other user in the conversation.
3. If the `convertView` is `null`, we inflate the appropriate layout based on the type.

4. Next, we pull the two text views, `messageText` and `dateText`, out of the `convertView`. We have to use the type value to make sure we use the correct resource IDs.

5. We set the appropriate text on both text views using the `message` object.

6. We return the `convertView`.

Now let's finish `MessagesActivity` by setting up the rest of the adapter. First, let's implement some member variables and the `OnCreate` method, as follows:

```
ListView listView;
EditText messageText;
Button sendButton;
Adapter adapter;

protected override void OnCreate(Bundle savedInstanceState)
{
  base.OnCreate(savedInstanceState);

  Title = viewModel.Conversation.UserName;
  SetContentView(Resource.Layout.Messages);
  listView = FindViewById<ListView>(Resource.Id.messageList);
  messageText = FindViewById<EditText>(Resource.Id.messageText);
  sendButton = FindViewById<Button>(Resource.Id.sendButton);

  listView.Adapter =
     adapter = new Adapter(this);

  sendButton.Click += async (sender, e) =>
  {
    viewModel.Text = messageText.Text;
    try
    {
      await viewModel.SendMessage();
      messageText.Text = string.Empty;
      adapter.NotifyDataSetInvalidated();
    }
    catch (Exception exc)
    {
      DisplayError(exc);
    }
  };
}
```

So far, this activity is fairly standard compared to our previous activities in this chapter. We also had to wire up the `Click` event of `sendButton` in `OnCreate` so that it sends the message and refreshes the list. We also used a trick to scroll the list view to the end by setting its selection to the last item.

Next, we'll need to implement `OnResume` to load the messages, invalidate the adapter, and then scroll the list view to the end, as follows:

```
protected async override void OnResume()
{
  base.OnResume();
  try
  {
    await viewModel.GetMessages();
    adapter.NotifyDataSetInvalidated();
    listView.SetSelection(adapter.Count);
  }
  catch (Exception exc)
  {
    DisplayError(exc);
  }
}
```

Last but not least, we need to modify `ConversationsActivity.cs`, so that it navigates forward when you tap on a row in the list view:

```
protected override void OnCreate(Bundle savedInstanceState)
{
  base.OnCreate(savedInstanceState);

  //Leave code here unmodified

  listView.ItemClick += (sender, e) =>
  {
    viewModel.Conversation = viewModel.Conversations[e.Position];
    StartActivity(typeof(MessagesActivity));
  };
}
```

So finally, if you compile and run the app, you will be able to navigate to the messages screen and add new messages to the list, as shown in the following screenshot:

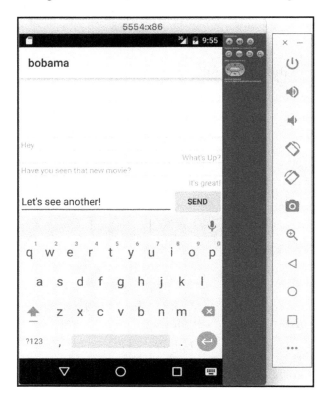

Summary

In this chapter, we started out by going over the basic settings in the Android Manifest file. Next, we implemented a custom `Application` class for setting up our `ServiceContainer`. We then went over the different types of Android layouts and implemented a login screen using native Android views. Next, we set up a menu in the Android action bar by using an Android layout and overriding a few built-in methods. We implemented the friends list screen, and learned the basics of `ListView` and adapters. Finally, we implemented the messages screen, and used the more advanced functionality available in list view adapters and layouts.

Upon completing this chapter, you will have a partially functional Android version of XamSnap. You will have gained some deeper understanding of the Android SDK and tools. You should be confident in developing your own Android applications using Xamarin. Take it upon yourself to implement the remaining screens that we did not cover in this chapter. If you get lost, feel free to review the full sample application included with this book. In the next chapter, we'll cover how to deploy to mobile devices and why it is very important to test your applications on real devices.

7
Deploying and Testing on Devices

Deploying to devices is both important and somewhat a hassle when you try it the first time. Certain issues will only happen on a mobile device, and cannot be reproduced in the iOS simulator or Android emulator. You can also test things that are only possible on real devices such as GPS, camera, memory limitations, or cellular network connectivity. There are also a few common pitfalls that exist when developing for Xamarin, which will only surface when testing on a physical device.

In this chapter, we will cover:

- iOS provisioning
- Android device settings for debugging
- The linker
- Ahead-of-time (AOT) compilation
- Common memory pitfalls with Xamarin

Before we begin this chapter, it is important to note that a valid iTunes account or iOS Developer Program membership is required to deploy to iOS devices. Feel free to go back to `Chapter 1`, *Xamarin Setup*, to walk through that process.

iOS provisioning

Apple has a strict process for deploying applications to iOS devices. While being quite convoluted and sometimes painful for developers, Apple can enable a certain level of security by preventing the average user from sideloading potentially malicious applications.

Before we can deploy our application to an iOS device, there are a few things we will need to set up in the **iOS Dev Center**. We will begin by creating an App ID or bundle ID for your account. This is the primary identifier for any iOS application.

Begin by navigating to http://developer.apple.com/account and perform the following steps:

1. Sign in with your developer account.
2. Click on **Certificates, IDs, & Profiles** on the right-hand-side navigation.
3. Click on **App IDs**.
4. Click on the plus button to add a new iOS App ID.
5. In the **Name** field, enter something meaningful, such as
   `YourCompanyNameWildcard`.
6. Select the **Wildcard App ID** radio button.
7. In the **Bundle ID** field, select a reverse domain styled name for your company, such as `com.yourcompanyname.*`.
8. Click on **Continue**.
9. Review the final setting and hit **Submit**.

Leave this webpage open, as we will be using it throughout the chapter.

We just registered a wildcard bundle ID for your account; use this as a prefix for all future applications you wish to identify with this account. Later, when you are preparing to deploy an app to the Apple App Store, you will create an **Explicit App ID** such as `com.yourcompanyname.yourapp`. This allows you to deploy the specific app to the store, while the wildcard ID is best used for deploying to devices for testing.

Next we need to locate the unique identifier on each device you plan to debug your application on. Apple requires each device to be registered under your account and has a limit of 110 devices per device type per developer (110 iPhones, iPads, iPods, Apple TVs, or Apple Watches). The only way to circumvent this requirement is to register for the iOS Developer Enterprise Program, which has a $299 yearly fee that is separate from the standard $99 developer fee.

Begin by launching Xcode and perform the following steps:

1. Click on **Window | Devices** in the top menu.
2. Plug in your target device with a USB cable.
3. On the left-hand-side navigation, you should see your device's name; select it.
4. Notice the **Identifier** value for your device. Copy it to your clipboard.

The following screenshot shows what your screen should look like with your device selected in Xcode:

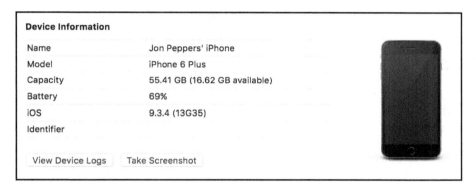

Return to `http://developer.apple.com/account`(hopefully, it is still open from earlier in the chapter) and perform the following steps:

1. Click on **Devices | All** on the left-hand-side navigation.
2. Click on the plus button in the top-right corner of the page.
3. Enter a meaningful name for your device and paste the **Identifier** from your clipboard into the **UDID** field.
4. Click on **Continue**.
5. Review the information you entered and hit **Register**.

Down the road, when your account is fully set up, you can just click on the **Use for Development** button in Xcode and skip this second set of steps.

The following screenshot shows what your device list should look like when complete:

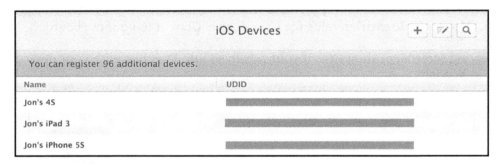

Next, we will need to generate a certificate to represent you as the developer for your account. Prior to Xcode 5, you had to create a certificate-signing request by using the **Keychain** app on your Mac. The newer versions of Xcode make things a lot easier by integrating a lot of this process into Xcode.

Open Xcode and perform the following steps:

1. Navigate to **Xcode** | **Preferences** in the menu at the top.
2. Select the **Accounts** tab.
3. Click on the plus button on the bottom-left and then click on **Add Apple ID**.
4. Enter the e-mail and password for your developer account.
5. Upon creating the account, click on **View Details** on the bottom-right.
6. Click on the **Download All** button on the bottom-left.
7. If this is a new account, Xcode will display a warning that no certificates exist yet. Check each box and click on **Request** to generate the certificates.

Xcode will now automatically create a developer certificate for your account and install it into your Mac's keychain.

The following screenshot shows what your screen will look after setting up your account:

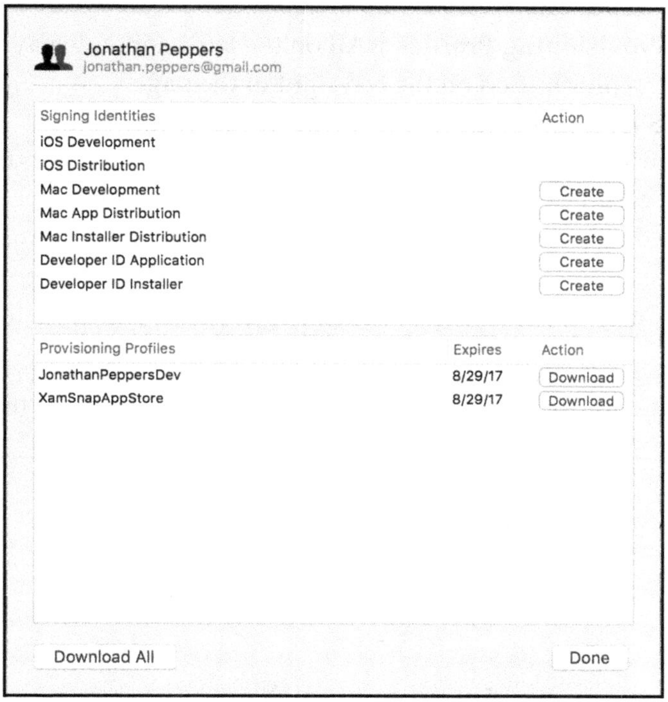

Next, we need to create a **provisioning profile**. This is the final file that allows applications to be installed on an iOS device. A provisioning profile contains an App ID, a list of device IDs, and, finally, a certificate for the developer. You must also have the private key of the developer certificate in your Mac's keychain to use a provisioning profile.

The following are a few types of provisioning profiles:

- **Development**: This is used for debug or release builds; you will actively use this type of profile when your applications are in development.
- **Ad Hoc**: This is used mainly for release builds; this type of certificate is great for beta testing or distribution to a small set of users. You can distribute to an unlimited number of users using this method with an enterprise developer account.
- **App Store**: This is used for release builds for submission to the App Store. You cannot deploy an app to your device using this certificate; it can only be used for store submission.

Let's return to http://developer.apple.com/apple and create a new provisioning profile by performing the following steps:

1. Click on **Provisioning Profiles | All** on the left-hand-side navigation.
2. Click on the plus button on the top-right of the page.
3. Select **iOS App Development** and click on **Continue**.
4. Select your wildcard App ID created earlier in the chapter and click on **Continue**.
5. Select the certificate we created earlier in the chapter and click on **Continue**.
6. Select the devices you want to deploy to and click on **Continue**.
7. Enter an appropriate **Profile Name**, such as YourCompanyDev.
8. Click on **Continue** and your provisioning profile will be created.

The following screenshot shows the new profile that you will end up with upon creation. Don't worry about downloading the file; we'll use Xcode to import the final profile.

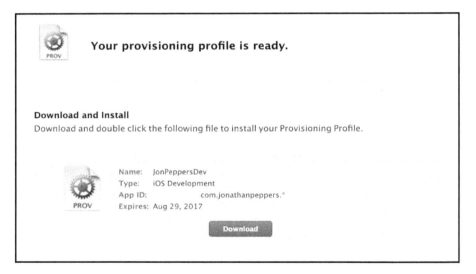

To import the provisioning profile, return to Xcode and perform the following steps:

1. Navigate to **Xcode | Preferences** in the menu at the top of the dialog.
2. Select the **Accounts** tab.
3. Select your account and click on **View Details**.
4. Click on the **Download All** button on the bottom-left.
5. After a few seconds, your provisioning profiles will appear.

Xcode should automatically include any provisioning profiles you have created on the Apple developer site. Xcode will also create a few profiles on its own.

In the latest version of Xamarin Studio, you can view these profiles, but will not be able to sync them. Navigate to **Xamarin Studio** | **Preferences** | **Developer Accounts** to view the provisioning profiles from Xamarin Studio. You can also see Xamarin's documentation on iOS provisioning on their documentation website at `http://developer.xamarin.com/guid` `es/ios/getting_started/device_provisioning/`.

Android device settings

Compared to the hassle of deploying your application on iOS devices, Android is a breeze. To deploy an application to a device, you merely have to set a few settings on the device. This is due to Android's openness in comparison to iOS. Android device debugging is turned off for most users, but it can be easily turned on by any user that wishes to have a try at writing Android applications.

Begin by opening the **Settings** application. You may have to locate this by looking through all the applications on the device, as follows:

1. Scroll down and click on the section labeled **Developer options**.
2. In the action bar at the top, you may have to toggle a switch to the **ON** position. This varies on each device.
3. Scroll down and check **USB Debugging**.
4. A warning confirmation will appear; click on **OK**.

 Note that some newer Android devices have made it a little more difficult for the average user to turn on USB debugging. You have to click on the **Developer options** item seven times to turn this option on.

The following screenshot shows what your device will look like during the process:

After enabling this option, all you have to do is plug in your device via USB and debug an Android application in Xamarin Studio. You will see your device listed in the **Select Device** dialog. Note that if you are on Windows or have a non-standard device, you may have to visit your device vendor's website to install drivers. Most Samsung and Nexus devices install their drivers automatically. On Android 4.3 and higher, there is also a confirmation dialog on the device that appears before beginning a USB debugging session.

The following screenshot shows what your device will look like for a Samsung Galaxy in the **Select Device** dialog. Xamarin Studio will display the model number, which is not always a name that you may recognize. You can view this model number in your device's settings.

Understanding the linker

To keep Xamarin applications small and lightweight for mobile devices, Xamarin has created a feature for their compiler called the **linker**. Its main purpose is to strip unused code out of the core Mono assemblies (such as `System.dll`) and platform-specific assemblies (`Mono.Android.dll` and `Xamarin.iOS.dll`); however, it can also give you the same benefits if set up to run on your own assemblies. Without running the linker, the entire Mono framework can be around 30 megabytes. This is why linking is enabled by default in device builds, which enables you to keep your applications small.

The linker uses static analysis to work through the various code paths in an assembly. If it determines that a method or class is never used, it removes the unused code from that assembly. This can be a time-consuming process, so builds running in the simulator skip this step by default.

Xamarin applications have the following three main settings for the linker:

- **Don't Link**: In this, the linker compilation step is skipped. This is best for builds running in the simulator or if you need to diagnose a potential issue with the linker.
- **Link SDK Assemblies Only**: In this, the linker will only be run on the core Mono assemblies such as `System.dll`, `System.Core.dll` and `System.Xml.dll`.
- **Link All Assemblies**: In this, the linker is run against all the assemblies in your application, which includes any class libraries or third party assemblies you are using.

These settings can be found in the **Project** options of any Xamarin.iOS or Xamarin.Android application. These settings are generally not present in class libraries as they are generally associated with an iOS or Android application that will be deployed.

The linker can also cause potential issues at runtime as there are cases in which its analysis determines incorrectly that a piece of code is unused. This can happen if you are using features in the `System.Reflection` namespace instead of accessing the method or property directly. This is one reason why it is important for you to test your application on physical devices, as linking is enabled for device builds.

To demonstrate this issue, let's look at the following code example:

```
//Just a simple class for holding info
public class Person
{
  public int Id { get; set; }
  public string Name { get; set; }
}

//Then somewhere later in your code
var person = new Person { Id = 1, Name = "Chuck Norris" };
var propInfo = person.GetType().GetProperty("Name");
string value = propInfo.GetValue(person) as string;
Console.WriteLine("Name: " + value);
```

Running the preceding code will work fine using the options for **Don't Link** or **Link SDK Assemblies Only**. However, if you try to run this when using **Link All Assemblies**, you will get an exception similar to the following:

```
Unhandled Exception:
System.ArgumentException: Get Method not found for 'Name'
    at System.Reflection.MonoProperty.GetValue (System.Object obj,
    BindingFlags invokeAttr, System.Reflection.Binder binder,
    System.Object[] index, System.Globalization.CultureInfo culture)
    at System.Reflection.PropertyInfo.GetValue (System.Object obj)
```

Since the `Name` property's getter was never used directly from code, the linker stripped it from the assembly. This caused the reflection code to fail at runtime.

Even though potential issues can arise in your code, the option of **Link All Assemblies** is still quite useful. There are a few optimizations that can only be performed in this mode, and Xamarin can reduce your application to the smallest possible size. If performance or a tiny download size is the requirement for your application, give this option a try. However, thorough testing should be performed to verify that no problems are caused by linking your assemblies.

To resolve issues in your code, Xamarin has included a complete set of workarounds to prevent specific parts of your code from being stripped away.

Some of the options include the following:

- Mark class members with `[Preserve]`; this will force the linker to include the attributed method, field, or property.
- Mark an entire class with `[Preserve(AllMembers=true)]`; this will preserve all code within the class.

- Mark an entire assembly with [assembly: Preserve]; this is an assembly-level attribute that will preserve all code contained within it.
- Skip an entire assembly by modifying **Additional mtouch arguments** in your project options; use --linkskip=System to skip an entire assembly. This can be used on assemblies that you do not have the source code for.
- Custom linking via an XML file, which is the best option when you need to skip linking on a specific class or method that you do not have the source code for. Use --xml=YourFile.xml in **Additional mtouch arguments**.

The following is a sample XML file demonstrating custom linking:

```
<linker>
  <assembly fullname="mscorlib">
    <type fullname="System.Environment">
      <field name="mono_corlib_version" />
      <method name="get_StackTrace" />
    </type>
  </assembly>
  <assembly fullname="My.Assembly.Name">
    <type fullname="MyTypeA" preserve="fields" />
      <method name=".ctor" />
    </type>
    <type fullname="MyTypeB" />
      <method signature="System.Void MyFunc(System.Int32 x)" />
      <field signature="System.String _myField" />
    </type>
  </assembly>
</linker>
```

Custom linking is the most complicated option and is usually the last resort. Luckily, most Xamarin applications will not have to work around many linker issues.

Understanding AOT compilation

The runtime behind Mono and .NET on Windows is based on a **just-in-time** (**JIT**) compiler. C# and other .NET languages are compiled into **Microsoft intermediate language** (**MSIL**). At runtime, MSIL is compiled into a native code (just in time) to run on whatever type of architecture is running your application. Xamarin.Android follows this exact pattern. However, due to Apple's restrictions on dynamically generated code, a **just-in-time** (**JIT**) compiler is not allowed on iOS.

To work around this restriction, Xamarin has developed a new option called **ahead-of-time (AOT)** compilation, in which your C# code is compiled into native, platform-specific machine code. In addition to making .NET possible on iOS, AOT has other benefits, such as a shorter startup time and potentially better performance.

AOT also has some limitations that are generally related to C# generics. To compile an assembly ahead of time, the compiler will need to run some static analysis against your code to determine the type information. Generics throw a wrench into this situation.

There are a few cases that are not supported with AOT, but are completely valid in C#. The first is a generic interface, as follows:

```
interface MyInterface<T>
{
   T GetMyValue();
}
```

The compiler cannot determine the classes that may implement this interface ahead of time, especially when multiple assemblies are involved. The second limitation is related to the first: you cannot override virtual methods that contain generic parameters or return values.

The following is a simple example:

```
class MyClass<T>
{
  public virtual T GetMyValue()
  {
    //Some code here
  }
}

class MySubClass : MyClass<int>
{
  public override int GetMyValue()
  {
    //Some code here
  }
}
```

Again, the static analysis of the compiler cannot determine which classes may override this method at compile time.

Another limitation is that you cannot use `DllImport` in a generic class, as shown in the following code:

```
class MyGeneric<T>
{
  [DllImport("MyImport")]
  public static void MyImport();
}
```

If you are not familiar with the language feature, `DllImport` is a way to call native C/C++ methods from C#. Using them inside generic classes is not supported.

These limitations are another good reason why testing on devices is important, since the preceding code will work fine on other platforms that can run C# code, but not Xamarin.iOS.

Avoiding common memory pitfalls

Memory on mobile devices is certainly not an unlimited commodity. Because of this, memory usage in your application can be much more important than on desktop applications. At times, you might find the need to use a memory profiler or improve your code to use memory more efficiently.

The following are the most common memory pitfalls:

- The **garbage collector** (**GC**) is unable to collect large objects fast enough to keep up with your application
- Your code inadvertently causes a memory leak
- A C# object is garbage collected, but is later attempted to be used by native code

Let's take a look at the first problem, where the GC cannot keep up. Let's say we have a Xamarin.iOS application with a button for sharing an image on Twitter, as follows:

```
twitterShare.TouchUpInside += (sender, e) =>
{
  var image = UImage.FromFile("YourLargeImage.png");
  //Share to Twitter
};
```

Now let's assume the image is a 10 MB image from the user's camera roll. If the user clicks on the button and cancels the Twitter post rapidly, there could be the possibility of your application running out of memory. iOS will commonly force apps using too much memory to close, and you don't want users to experience this with your app.

The best solution is to call `Dispose` on the image when you are finished with it, as follows:

```
var image = UImage.FromFile("YourLargeImage.png");
//Share to Twitter
image.Dispose();
```

An even better approach would be to take advantage of the C# `using` statement, as follows:

```
using(var image = UImage.FromFile("YourLargeImage.png"))
{
  //Share to Twitter
}
```

The C# `using` statement will automatically call `Dispose` in a `try-finally` block, so the object will get disposed of even if an exception is thrown. I recommend taking advantage of the `using` statement for any `IDisposable` class, where possible. It is not always necessary for small objects, such as `NSString`, but it is always a good idea for larger, more heavyweight `UIKit` objects.

 A similar situation can occur in Android with the `Bitmap` class. Although slightly different, it is best to call the `Dispose` method on this class, the same as you would with `UIImage` on iOS.

A memory leak is the next potential issue. C#, being a managed, garbage-collected language, prevents a lot of memory leaks, but not all of them. The most common leaks in C# are caused by events.

Let's assume we have a static class with an event, as follows:

```
static class MyStatic
{
  public static event EventHandler MyEvent;
}
```

Now, let's say we need to subscribe to the event from an iOS controller, as follows:

```
public override void ViewDidLoad()
{
  base.ViewDidLoad();

  MyStatic.MyEvent += (sender, e) =>
  {
    //Do something
  };
}
```

The problem here is that the static class will hold a reference to the controller until the event is unsubscribed. This is a situation that a lot of developers might miss. To fix this issue on iOS, I would subscribe to the event in `ViewWillAppear` and unsubscribe from `ViewWillDisappear`. On Android, use `OnStart` and `OnStop`, or `OnPause` and `OnResume`.

You would correctly implement this event, as follows:

```
public override void ViewWillAppear()
{
  base.ViewWillAppear();
  MyStatic.MyEvent += OnMyEvent;
}

public override void ViewWillDisappear()
{
  base.ViewWillDisappear ();
  MyStatic.MyEvent -= OnMyEvent;
}
```

However, an event is not a surefire cause of a memory leak. Subscribing to the `TouchUpInside` event on a button inside the `ViewDidLoad` method, for example, is just fine. Since the button lives in memory just as long as the controller, everything can be garbage collected without causing a problem.

For the final issue, the garbage collector can sometimes remove a C# object; later, an Objective-C object attempts to access it.

The following is an example of adding a button to `UITableViewCell`:

```
public override UITableViewCell GetCell(
    UITableView tableView, NSIndexPath indexPath)
{
  var cell = tableView.DequeueReusableCell("MyCell");
  //Remaining cell setup here

  var button = UIButton.FromType(UIButtonType.InfoDark);
  button.TouchUpInside += (sender, e) =>
  {
    //Do something
  };
  cell.AccessoryView = button;
  return cell;
}
```

We add the built-in info button as an accessory view to the cell. The problem here is that the button will be garbage collected, but its Objective-C counterpart will remain in use as it is displayed on the screen. If you click on the button after a period of time, you will get a crash that looks something like the following:

```
mono-rt: Stacktrace:
mono-rt:    at <unknown>
mono-rt:    at (wrapper managed-to-native)
MonoTouch.UIKit.UIApplication.UIApplicationMain
   (int,string[],intptr,intptr)
mono-rt:    at MonoTouch.UIKit.UIApplication.Main
(string[],string,string)
   ... Continued ...
=================================================================
Got a SIGSEGV while executing native code. This usually indicates
a fatal error in the mono runtime or one of the native libraries
used by your application.
=================================================================
```

It is not the most descriptive error message, but, in general, you know that something went wrong in the native Objective-C code. To resolve the issue, create a custom subclass of UITableViewCell and create a dedicated member variable for the button, as follows:

```
public class MyCell : UITableViewCell
{
  UIButton button;

  public MyCell()
  {
    button = UIButton.FromType(UIButtonType.InfoDark);
    button.TouchUpInside += (sender, e) =>
    {
      //Do something
    };
    AccessoryView = button;
  }
}
```

Now, your GetCell implementation will look something like the following:

```
public override UITableViewCell GetCell(
   UITableView tableView, NSIndexPath indexPath)
{
  var cell = tableView.DequeueReusableCell("MyCell") as MyCell;
  //Remaining cell setup here
  return cell;
}
```

Since the button is not a local variable, it will no longer be garbage collected sooner than needed. A crash is avoided, and, in some ways, this code is a bit cleaner. Similar situations can happen on Android with the interaction between C# and Java; however, it is less likely, since both are garbage-collected languages.

Summary

In this chapter, we started out learning the process of setting up iOS provision profiles to deploy to iOS devices. Next, we looked at the required device settings for deploying your application to an Android device. We discovered the Xamarin linker, and how it can make your applications smaller and more performant. We went over the various settings for resolving problems caused by your code and the linker, and we explained AOT compilation on iOS and the limitations that occur. Finally, we covered the most common memory pitfalls that can occur with Xamarin applications.

Testing your Xamarin application on mobile devices is important for various reasons. Some bugs are only displayed on the device due to the platform limitations that Xamarin has to work around. Your PC is much more powerful, so you will see different performance using the simulator compared to on a physical device. In the next chapter, we'll create a real web service using Windows Azure to drive our XamChat application. We will use a feature called Azure Mobile Services, and implement push notifications on iOS and Android.

8
Contacts, Camera, and Location

Some of the most vital features used by mobile applications today are based on the new types of data that can be collected by our devices. Features such as a device's GPS location and camera are staples in modern applications such as Instagram or Twitter. It's difficult to develop an application and not use some of these functionalities. So, let's explore our options for taking advantage of this functionality with Xamarin.

In this chapter, we will do the following:

- Introduce the Xamarin.Mobile library
- Read the address book on Android and iOS
- Retrieve the GPS location of our device
- Pull photos from the camera and photo library

Introducing Xamarin.Mobile

To simplify the development of these features across multiple platforms, Xamarin has developed a library called **Xamarin.Mobile**. It delivers a single API for accessing the contacts, GPS location, heading of the screen, camera, and photo library for iOS, Android, and even Windows platforms. It also takes advantage of **Task Parallel Libraries** (**TPL**) to deliver a modern C# API that will make developers more productive than their native alternatives would. This gives you the ability to write nice, clean, asynchronous code using the `async` and `await` keywords in C#. You can also reuse the same code in iOS and Android, apart from a few differences that are required by the Android platform.

To install Xamarin.Mobile, open the **Xamarin Component Store** in **Xamarin Studio** and add the **Xamarin.Mobile** component to a project, as shown in the following screenshot:

Before we dig further into using Xamarin.Mobile, let's review the namespaces and functionality available with the library:

- `Xamarin.Contacts`: This contains classes that enable you to interact with the full address book. It includes everything from the contact's photo, phone numbers, address, e-mail, website, and so on.
- `Xamarin.Geolocation`: This, combined with the accelerometer, gives you access to the device's GPS location, including the altitude, heading, longitude, latitude, and speed. You can track the device's position explicitly or listen for GPS position changes over time.
- `Xamarin.Media`: This grants access to the device's cameras (if there are more than one) and built-in photo library. This is an easy way to add photo selection capabilities to any application.

Xamarin.Mobile is an open source project with the standard Apache 2.0 license. You can contribute to the project or submit issues to the GitHub page at https://github.com/xamarin/Xamarin.Mobile. Feel free to use Xamarin.Mobile in your applications, or fork and modify it for your own purposes.

In this chapter, we will be adding lots of features to the XamSnap sample application, built in earlier chapters. You may wish to visit `Chapter 6`, *XamSnap for Android*, if needed, or refer to the sample source code included with this book.

Accessing contacts

To begin our exploration of what Xamarin.Mobile offers, let's access the address book within a Xamarin application. Let's improve the add friend feature of XamSnap by loading friends from the user's contact list. Make sure to add Xamarin.Mobile to the project from the Component Store for both the iOS and Android projects.

Navigate to the `XamSnap` portable class library. First, we will need to split apart the `IWebService` interface, by moving one method to a new `IFriendService` interface:

```
public interface IFriendService
{
    Task<User[]> GetFriends(string userName);
}
```

Next, in `FriendViewModel`, we will need to use the new `IFriendService` interface instead of the old one:

```
private IFriendService friendService =
  ServiceContainer.Resolve<IFriendService>();

public async Task GetFriends()
{
  //previous code here, use 'friendService' instead of 'service'
  Friends = await friendService.GetFriends(settings.User.Name);
}
```

Now, we need to implement IFriendService in the iOS project to allow it to load from a device's contact list. Navigate to the XamSnap.iOS project and add a new class implementing IFriendService:

```
public class ContactsService : IFriendService
{
  public async Task<User[]> GetFriends(string userName)
  {
    var book = new Xamarin.Contacts.AddressBook();
    await book.RequestPermission();

    var users = new List<User>();
    foreach (var contact in book)
    {
      users.Add(new User
      {
        Name = contact.DisplayName,
      });
    }
    return users.ToArray();
  }
}
```

In order to use Xamarin.Mobile to load contacts, you must first create an AddressBook object. Next, we have to call RequestPermissions in order to ask the user for permission to access the address book. This is an important step, since it is required by iOS devices before an application can access the user's contacts. This prevents potentially nefarious applications from retrieving contacts without the user's knowledge.

Next, we use foreach over the AddressBook object and create instances of the User object that our existing application already understands. This is a great example of how the MVVM design pattern is great at separating layers. When we swap out logic at the model layer, the UI continues to work properly without any changes.

Next, we need to modify our AppDelegate.cs file to use our ContactsService as the IFriendService interface:

```
ServiceContainer.Register<IFriendService>(
  () => new ContactsService());
```

If you were to compile and run the application at this point, you would be greeted by the standard iOS popup requesting access to contacts, as shown in the following screenshot:

If you accidentally hit **Don't Allow**, you can change this setting by navigating to **Settings | Privacy | Contacts** on the device. In the iOS Simulator, you can also reset all privacy prompts in the simulator by closing the application and going to **Settings | General | Reset | Reset Location & Privacy**.

If our app is granted the correct access, we should be able to see a list of contacts without modifying any code in the UI layer of our application. The following screenshot shows the default list of contacts in the iOS Simulator:

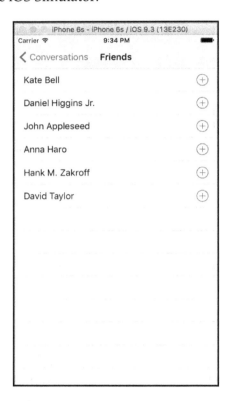

Retrieving contacts on Android

In a very similar fashion, we can retrieve a list of contacts in Android with Xamarin.Mobile. All of the APIs in Xamarin.Mobile are identical in Android, with the exception of the requirement to pass `Android.Content.Context` in a few places. This is because many native Android APIs require a reference to the current activity (or to another context such as `Application`) in order to function properly. To begin, create a standard Android Application project by navigating to **Android** | **Android Application** in Xamarin Studio. Make sure to add Xamarin.Mobile to the project from the Component Store.

Add an Android equivalent of the `IFriendService` as follows:

```
public class ContactsService : IFriendService
{
  public async Task<User[]> GetFriends(string userName)
  {
    var book = new
        Xamarin.Contacts.AddressBook(Application.Context);
    await book.RequestPermission();

    var users = new List<User>();
    foreach (var contact in book)
    {
      users.Add(new User
      {
        Name = contact.DisplayName,
      });
    }
    return users.ToArray();
  }
}
```

This code, calling Xamarin.Mobile, is identical to what we did on the code for iOS, except that here, `Application.Context` had to be passed for the Android `Context` in the constructor for `AddressBook`. Our code changes are complete; however, if you ran the application right now, an exception would be thrown. Android requires permission in the manifest file, which will notify the user of its access to the address book when downloaded from Google Play.

We must modify the `AndroidManifest.xml` file and declare one permission as follows:

1. Open the project options for the Android project.
2. Select the **Android Application** tab under **Build**.
3. Under the **Required permissions** section, check **ReadContacts**.
4. Click on **OK** to save your changes.

Now if you run the application, you will get a list of all the contacts on the device, as shown in the following screenshot:

Looking up GPS location

Using Xamarin.Mobile to track a user's GPS location is as simple as accessing their contacts. There is a similar process for setting up access on iOS and Android, but in the case of location, you don't have to request permission from code. iOS will automatically show the standard alert requesting permission. Android, on the other hand, merely requires a manifest setting.

As an example, let's add functionality to our XamSnap application that tags GPS location to messages within a chat conversation. You can think of this as tagging a location to a photo, as in other apps. Make sure to add Xamarin.Mobile to the project from the Component Store.

First, let's implement a `Location` class for storing latitude and longitude:

```
public class Location
{
    public double Latitude { get; set; }
    public double Longitude { get; set; }
}
```

Next, let's add a `Location` property to the `Message` class:

```
public Location Location { get; set; }
```

Now, let's create a new `ILocationService` interface for querying a GPS location:

```
public interface ILocationService
{
    Task<Location> GetCurrentLocation();
}
```

We now need to update the `MessageViewModel` class to use the location service and tag the GPS location on new messages:

```
//As a member variable
private ILocationService locationService =
  ServiceContainer.Resolve<ILocationService>();

//Then in SendMessage()
var location = await locationService.GetCurrentLocation();
var message = await service.SendMessage(new Message
{
    UserName = settings.User.Name,
    Conversation = Conversation.Id,
    Text = Text,
    Location = location,
});
```

Next, let's implement the `ILocationService` interface for iOS. Create a new class in the iOS project:

```
public class LocationService : ILocationService
{
  private const int Timeout = 3000;
  private Geolocator _geolocator;

  public async Task<Location> GetCurrentLocation()
  {
    try
    {
```

```
    //NOTE: wait until here to create Geolocator
    //  so that the iOS prompt appears on GetCurrentLocation()
    if (_geolocator == null)
      _geolocator = new Geolocator();

    var location = await _geolocator.GetPositionAsync(Timeout);

    Console.WriteLine("GPS location: {0},{1}",
      location.Latitude, location.Longitude);

    return new Location
    {
      Latitude = location.Latitude,
      Longitude = location.Longitude,
    };
  }
  catch (Exception exc)
  {
    Console.WriteLine("Error finding GPS location: " + exc);

    //If anything goes wrong, just return null
    return null;
  }
 }
}
```

What we did here was to first create a `Geolocator` object if needed. This delays the iOS permission popup until you actually go to send a message. We then used `async/await` to query for a GPS location with a three second timeout. We logged the location that was found and created a new `Location` object for use in the rest of our application. If any errors occurred, we made sure to log them and return `null` for our instance of `Location`.

Next, register our new service in `AppDelegate.cs`:

```
ServiceContainer.Register<ILocationService>(
    () => new LocationService());
```

Finally, there is a setting in our `Info.plist` file that is required by iOS for accessing a user's location and that also gives the developer the option to display a message in the permission popup.

Open the `Info.plist` file and change it as follows:

1. Click the **Source** tab.
2. Click the plus button on the **Add new entry** row.
3. In the dropdown, choose **Location When In Use Usage Description**.
4. Enter text for the user in the **Value** field.

If you compile and run the application, you should see an iOS permission prompt when adding a new message, as shown in the following screenshot:

If you watch the console log in Xamarin Studio, you will be able to see the GPS coordinates being added to the `Message` object. For this to actually work, you will have to deploy to a physical iOS device to see the GPS location returned.

Implementing GPS location on Android

Just as in the previous section, using Xamarin.Mobile for GPS location is almost identical to the APIs we used in iOS. First, we will need to create an `ILocationService` as before, only needing to change one line of code from that we created for iOS:

```
if (_geolocator == null)
  _geolocator = new Geolocator(Application.Context);
```

Then, also register our new service in `Application.cs`:

```
ServiceContainer.Register<ILocationService>(
  () => new LocationService());
```

Again, this looks identical to the code for iOS, except for the constructor for `Geolocator`. If you ran the application at this point, it would start with no errors. However, no events would be fired from the `Geolocator` object. We first need to add permission to access the location from the Android Manifest file. It is also a good idea to start the locator in `OnResume` and stop it in `OnPause`. This will conserve the battery by stopping the GPS location when this activity is no longer on the screen.

Let's create an `AndroidManifest.xml` file and declare two permissions, as follows:

1. Open the project options for the Android project.
2. Select the **Android Application** tab under **Build**.
3. Click on **Add Android manifest**.
4. Under the **Required permissions** section, check **AccessCoarseLocation** and **AccessFineLocation**.
5. Click on **OK** to save your changes.

Now if you compile and run the application, you will get the GPS location tagged to new messages sent. Most Android emulators have an option for emulating GPS location. The x86 HAXM emulator is found under the dots menu at the bottom, then **Extended Controls | Location**, as shown in the following screenshot:

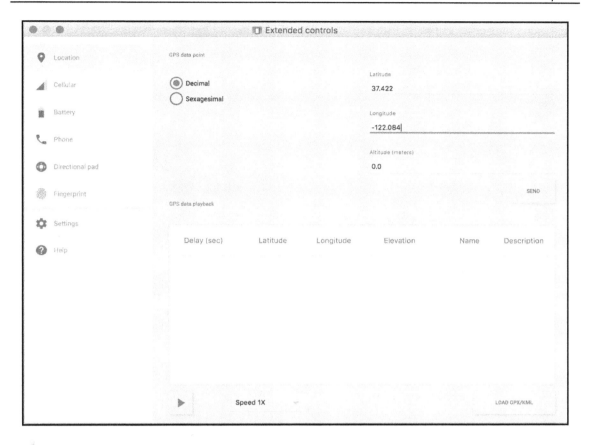

Accessing the photo library and camera

The last major feature of Xamarin.Mobile is the ability to access photos in order to give users the ability to add their own content to your applications. Using a class called `MediaPicker`, you can pull photos from the device's camera or photo library and optionally display your own UI for the operation.

Let's modify `MessageViewModel` to support photos. First, add the following property:

```
public string Image { get; set; }
```

Next, we need to modify the following lines in the `SendMessage` method:

```
if (string.IsNullOrEmpty(Text) && string.IsNullOrEmpty(Image))
    throw new Exception("Message is blank.");

//Then further down
var message = await service.SendMessage(new Message
{
    UserName = settings.User.Name,
    Conversation = Conversation.Id,
    Text = Text,
    Image = Image,
    Location = location,
});

//Clear our variables
Text =
    Image = null;
```

Next, we will need to modify the UI layer to prompt for photos. Open `MessagesController.cs` and add the following variables to the top of the class:

```
UIBarButtonItem photo;
MediaPicker picker;
```

In the `ViewDidLoad` method, we will need to set up the `MediaPicker` and a new `UIBarButtonItem` to choose a photo:

```
picker = new MediaPicker();
photo = new UIBarButtonItem(UIBarButtonSystemItem.Camera,
  (sender, e) =>
  {
    //In case the keyboard is up
    message.ResignFirstResponder();

    var actionSheet = new UIActionSheet("Choose photo?");
    actionSheet.AddButton("Take Photo");
    actionSheet.AddButton("Photo Library");
    actionSheet.AddButton("Cancel");
    actionSheet.Clicked += OnActionSheetClicked;
    actionSheet.CancelButtonIndex = 2;
    actionSheet.ShowFrom(photo, true);
  });
```

We are using the `UIActionSheet` class here to prompt the user to decide whether they want to take a new photo or open an existing one. Now let's implement the `OnActionSheetClicked` method:

```
async void OnActionSheetClicked(
  object sender, UIButtonEventArgs e)
{
  MediaPickerController controller = null;
  try
  {
    if (e.ButtonIndex == 0)
    {
      if (!picker.IsCameraAvailable)
      {
        new UIAlertView("Oops!",
          "Sorry, camera not available on this device!", null,
          "Ok").Show();
        return;
      }

      controller = picker.GetTakePhotoUI(
        new StoreCameraMediaOptions());
      PresentViewController(controller, true, null);

      var file = await controller.GetResultAsync();
      messageViewModel.Image = file.Path;
      Send();
    }
    else if (e.ButtonIndex == 1)
    {
      controller = picker.GetPickPhotoUI();
      PresentViewController(controller, true, null);

      var file = await controller.GetResultAsync();
      messageViewModel.Image = file.Path;
      Send();
    }
  }
  catch (TaskCanceledException)
  {
    //Means the user just cancelled
  }
  finally
  {
    controller?.DismissViewController(true, null);
  }
}
```

Using `MediaPicker` is pretty straightforward; you merely have to call `GetTakePhotoUI` or `GetPickPhotoUI` to retrieve a `MediaPickerController` instance. Then, you can call `PresentViewController` to display the controller modally over the top of the current controller. After calling `GetResultAsync` we use the resulting `MediaFile` object to pass the path of the photo to our ViewModel layer. It is also necessary to use a `try-catch` block, in case the user cancels and calls `DismissViewController` to hide the modal.

Next, we need to modify `UITableViewSource` to display photos:

```
public override UITableViewCell GetCell(
  UITableView tableView, NSIndexPath indexPath)
  {
    var message = messageViewModel.Messages[indexPath.Row];
    bool isMyMessage = message.UserName == settings.User.Name;
    var cell = tableView.DequeueReusableCell(
      isMyMessage ? MyCellName : TheirCellName);
    cell.TextLabel.Text = message.Text ?? string.Empty;
    cell.ImageView.Image = string.IsNullOrEmpty(message.Image) ?
      null : UIImage.FromFile(message.Image);
    return cell;
  }
```

One last case we need to handle is in the `ViewWillAppear` method:

```
//Just after subscribing to IsBusyChanged
if (PresentedViewController != null)
  return;
```

If we did not make this change, the list of photos would refresh after choosing a photo, which could cause some odd behavior.

You should now be able to run the app and select a photo to be viewed on the screen. The following screenshot shows a nice default photo from the iOS simulator that I selected from the photo library:

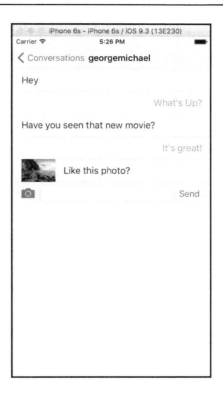

Accessing photos on Android

In comparison to iOS, we have to use a slightly different pattern on Android to retrieve photos from the camera or photo library. A common pattern in Android is that it calls `StartActivityForResult` to launch an activity from another application. When this activity is completed, `OnActivityResult` will be called to notify your activity that the action is complete. Because of this, Xamarin.Mobile could not use the same APIs on Android as on iOS.

First, let's modify our Android layouts to handle photos. Add a new `ImageButton` in `Messages.axml` before `EditText`, as follows:

```
<ImageButton
    android:layout_width="wrap_content"
    android:layout_height="wrap_content"
    android:id="@+id/photoButton"
    android:layout_alignParentLeft="true"
    android:src="@android:drawable/ic_menu_camera" />
```

Then add the `android:layout_toRightOf="@+id/photoButton"` attribute to `EditText`.

Next, we need to modify both `MyMessageListItem` and `TheirMessageListItem` as follows:

```
<!-MyMessageListItem-->
<ImageView
    android:layout_width="wrap_content"
    android:layout_height="wrap_content"
    android:id="@+id/myMessageImage" />
<TextView    android:text="Message"
    android:layout_width="wrap_content"
    android:layout_height="wrap_content"
    android:id="@+id/myMessageText"
    android:layout_margin="3dp"
    android:textColor="@android:color/holo_blue_bright"
    android:layout_toRightOf="@id/myMessageImage" />
<!-TheirMessageListItem-->
<ImageView
    android:layout_width="wrap_content"
    android:layout_height="wrap_content"
    android:id="@+id/theirMessageImage" />
<TextView
    android:text="Message"
    android:layout_width="wrap_content"
    android:layout_height="wrap_content"
    android:id="@+id/theirMessageText"
    android:layout_margin="3dp"
    android:textColor="@android:color/holo_green_light"
    android:layout_alignParentRight="true" />
```

In both of these cases, it is a lot easier to just modify the Android XML, as the designer is sometimes a bit finicky when adding new views to the left or right of existing views.

Now let's add a couple of member variables to the top of `MessagesActivity.cs` as follows:

```
MediaPicker picker;
ImageButton photoButton;
bool choosingPhoto;
```

Next, let's rearrange the `OnCreate` method as follows:

```
protected override void OnCreate(Bundle savedInstanceState)
{
  base.OnCreate(savedInstanceState);
```

```
    Title = viewModel.Conversation.UserName;
    SetContentView(Resource.Layout.Messages);
    listView = FindViewById<ListView>(Resource.Id.messageList);
    messageText = FindViewById<EditText>(Resource.Id.messageText);
    sendButton = FindViewById<Button>(Resource.Id.sendButton);
    photoButton = FindViewById<ImageButton>(
        Resource.Id.photoButton);

    picker = new MediaPicker(this);

    listView.Adapter =
        adapter = new Adapter(this);
    sendButton.Click += (sender, e) => Send();
    photoButton.Click += (sender, e) =>
    {
        var dialog = new AlertDialog.Builder(this)
            .SetTitle("Choose photo?")
            .SetPositiveButton("Take Photo", OnTakePhoto)
            .SetNegativeButton("Photo Library", OnChoosePhoto)
            .SetNeutralButton("Cancel", delegate { })
            .Create();
        dialog.Show();
    };
}

async void Send()
{
    viewModel.Text = messageText.Text;
    try
    {
        await viewModel.SendMessage();
        messageText.Text = string.Empty;
        adapter.NotifyDataSetInvalidated();
    }
    catch (Exception exc)
    {
        DisplayError(exc);
    }
}
```

What we are doing here is creating an AlertDialog when the photoButton is clicked.
This is identical to what we did on iOS, giving the option for the user to either take a photo
or choose one from their existing photo library. We have also moved the click handler of
sendButton to a Send method so we can reuse it.

Now, let's implement the `OnTakePhoto` and `OnChoosePhoto` methods needed:

```
void OnTakePhoto(object sender, EventArgs e)
{
    var intent = picker.GetTakePhotoUI(
      new StoreCameraMediaOptions());
    choosingPhoto = true;
    StartActivityForResult(intent, 1);
}

void OnChoosePhoto(object sender, EventArgs e)
{
    var intent = picker.GetPickPhotoUI();
    choosingPhoto = true;
    StartActivityForResult(intent, 1);
}
```

In each case, we make a call to `GetPickPhotoUI` or `GetTakePhotoUI` in order to get an instance of an Android `Intent` object. This object is used to start new activities within an application. `StartActivityForResult` will also start the `Intent` object, expecting a result to be returned from the new activity.

Next, we need to implement `OnActivityResult` in order to handle what will happen when the new activity is completed:

```
protected async override void OnActivityResult(
   int requestCode, Result resultCode, Intent data)
{
    if (resultCode == Result.Ok)
    {
        var file = await data.GetMediaFileExtraAsync(this);
        viewModel.Image = file.Path;
        Send();
    }
}
```

If this is successful, we retrieve a `MediaFile` and pass its path to our ViewModel layer. We call our `Send` method that we set up earlier, which sends the message.

One other detail we need is to add the following code to our `OnResume` method:

```
if (choosingPhoto)
{
    choosingPhoto = false;
    return;
}
```

This prevents some odd behavior when the user navigates away to a new activity to choose a photo and then returns. It is very similar to what we had to do on iOS.

For these changes to work, we need to modify our `AndroidManifest.xml` file and declare two permissions as follows:

1. Open the project options for the Android project.
2. Select the **Android Application** tab under **Build**.
3. Click on **Add Android manifest**.
4. Under the **Required permissions** section, check **Camera** and **WriteExternalStorage**.
5. Click on **OK** to save your changes.

You should now be able to run the application and send photos as messages, as shown in the following screenshot:

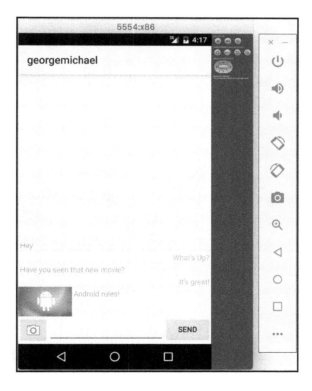

Summary

In this chapter, we discovered the Xamarin.Mobile library and how it can accelerate common tasks in a cross-platform way. We retrieved contacts from the address book and set up GPS location updates over time. Lastly, we loaded photos from the camera and photo library.

After completing this chapter, you should have a complete grasp of the Xamarin.Mobile library and the common functionality it provides for cross-platform development. It gives clean, modern APIs that offer `async/await` functionality that can be accessed across iOS, Android, and Windows Phone. Accessing contacts, GPS, and photos across platforms is very straightforward with Xamarin.Mobile.

In the next chapter, we'll create a real web service using Windows Azure to drive our XamSnap application. We will use a feature called Azure Functions and implement push notifications on iOS and Android.

9
Web Services with Push Notifications

Modern mobile applications are defined by their network connectivity. A mobile app that does not interact with a web server is both a rare find and potentially a boring application. In this book, we'll use the **Windows Azure** cloud platform to implement a server-side backend for our XamSnap application. We'll use a feature called **Azure Functions**, which is an excellent fit as a simple backend for our application and can send push notifications via **Azure Notification Hubs**. Once we are done with this chapter, our XamSnap sample application will be much closer to being a real application and will allow its users to interact with one another.

In this chapter, we will cover the following topics:

- The services offered by Windows Azure
- Setting up your Azure account
- Azure Functions as a backend for XamSnap
- Implementing a real web service for XamSnap
- Writing client-side code for calling Azure Functions
- Using the Apple Push Notification service
- Sending notifications with Google Cloud Messaging

Learning Windows Azure

Windows Azure is an excellent cloud platform released by Microsoft in 2010. Azure provides both **Infrastructure as a Service (IaaS)** and **Platform as a Service (PaaS)** for building modern web applications and services. This means that it provides you the access directly to virtual machines within which you can deploy any operating system or software of your choice. This is known as IaaS. Azure also provides multiple platforms for building applications, such as **Azure Web Apps** or **SQL Azure**. These platforms are known as PaaS, since you deploy your software at a high level and do not have to deal directly with virtual machines or manage software upgrades.

Let's go over the following more common services provided by Windows Azure:

- **Virtual Machines**: Azure provides you the access to virtual machines of all sizes. You can install practically any operating system of your choice; there are many premade distributions to choose from within Azure's gallery.
- **Web Apps**: You can deploy any type of website that will run in Microsoft **IIS**, from ASP .NET sites to **PHP** or **Node.js**.
- **SQL Azure**: This is a cloud-based version of Microsoft SQL Server, which is a fully featured **RDMS (Regional Database Management System)** for storing data.
- **Mobile Apps**: This is a simple platform for building web services for mobile apps. It uses **SQL Azure** for backend storage and a simple JavaScript scripting system based on Node.js for adding business logic.
- **Azure Functions**: The first product of Windows Azure supporting the new "serverless" architecture that is becoming today's new buzzword. You can develop simple APIs, background jobs, webhooks, and so on in a variety of languages directly in the web browser. Azure will automatically scale your function based on incoming requests.
- **Storage**: Azure provides **blob storage**, a method for storing binary files and **table storage**, which is a **NoSQL** solution for persisting data.
- **Service bus**: This is a cloud-based solution for creating queues to facilitate communication between other cloud services. It also includes notification hubs as a simple way to provide push notifications to mobile apps.
- **Notification Hubs**: A simple way to send push notifications to different platforms such as Android, iOS, and Windows devices.
- **DocumentDB**: A fully featured NoSQL data storage comparable to other NoSQL databases such as **MongoDB**.
- **HDInsight**: A version of Apache Hadoop running in Windows Azure for managing extremely large data sets, which also could be called big data.

Apart from these services, there are many more and new ones actively being developed. We will use Azure Functions, and also leverage Azure Storage Tables, to build our web service for XamSnap. You can visit http://windowsazure.com for a full rundown of pricing and services offered.

In this book, we chose to demonstrate a solution using Windows Azure as a web service backend for XamSnap, since it is complementary with C#, Visual Studio, and other Microsoft tools. However, there are many more choices out there besides Azure, which you may want to look at. Choosing Xamarin does not limit the types of web service your applications can interact with.

Here are a few more common ones:

- **Firebase**: This service by Google provides a product similar to that of Azure Mobile Apps, complete with data storage and push notifications. You can get more information at https://firebase.google.com.
- **Urban airship**: This service provides push notifications for mobile apps across multiple platforms. You can get more information at http://urbanairship.com.
- **Amazon Web Services**: This service is a complete cloud solution that is equivalent to Windows Azure. It has everything you need to deploy applications in the cloud with total virtual machine support. There is also a feature called **AWS Mobile Hub**, tailored specifically for mobile development. You can get more information at http://aws.amazon.com.

Additionally, you can develop your own web services with on-premises web servers or inexpensive hosting services using the languages and technologies of your choice.

Setting up your Azure account

To start developing with Windows Azure, you can subscribe to a free one-month trial along with $200 in free Azure credit. To go along with this, many of its services have free tiers that give you lower performance versions. So, if your trial expires, you can continue your development at little or no cost, depending on the services you are using.

Begin by navigating to http://azure.microsoft.com/en-us/free and then carry out the following steps:

1. Click on the **Start Free** link.
2. Sign in with a Windows Live ID.
3. For security purposes, verify your account via your phone or a text message.

4. Enter the payment information. This is only used if you exceed your spending limits. You won't accidentally spend beyond budget by developing your app-it is not common to accidentally spend money until real users are interacting with your services.

5. Check **I agree** to the policies and click on **Sign Up**.

6. Review the final setting and click on **Submit**.

If all the required information is entered correctly, you will now finally have access to your Azure account. You can click the **PORTAL** link in the top-right corner of the page to access your account. In the future, you can manage your Azure services at http://portal.azure.com.

The Azure Portal uses a set of panels named blades, to quickly navigate and drill deeper into more detailed information, as shown in the following screenshot:

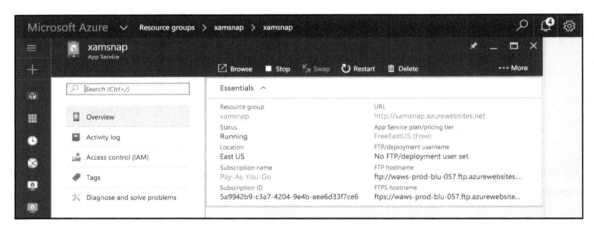

This concludes your sign up for Windows Azure. It is pretty simple compared to the Apple and Google Play developer programs. Feel free to play around, but don't be too worried about spending money. Azure has free versions of most services and also delivers a good amount of bandwidth for free. You can get more information on pricing at http://azure.microsoft.com/en-us/pricing.

Note that there are a lot of misconceptions about Windows Azure being expensive. You can do all of your development for an application on the free tier without spending a dime. When putting applications into production, you can easily scale up or down on the number of VM instances to keep your costs under control. In general, you will not be spending much money if you do not have a lot of users. Likewise, you should be earning plenty of revenue if you happen to have lots of users.

Exploring Azure Functions

For the server side of XamSnap, we'll use Azure Functions along with Azure Storage Tables to provide backend storage to the application. Azure Functions is a simple solution to accelerate development for server-side applications that can leverage all features of Windows Azure. We will use the standard `HttpClient` class found in the .NET base class library for interacting with the service from C#.

A few neat features of Azure Functions are as follows:

- You can write functions in a variety of programming languages such as JavaScript, C#, Python, and PHP, as well as some scripting languages such as Batch, Bash, and PowerShell
- Azure Functions integrates with Visual Studio Team Services, Bitbucket, and GitHub for **Continuous Integration (CI)** scenarios
- You can set up authentication easily with Azure Active Directory, Windows Live ID, Facebook, Google, and Twitter
- Functions can be triggered via HTTP, a schedule or timer, Azure Queue, and so on
- Azure Functions is truly serverless and can scale dynamically for large volumes of data

You can see why using Azure Functions is a good choice for simple mobile applications. The benefits of accelerated development and the many features it provides are a great fit for our XamSnap sample application.

Navigating to your account at http://portal.azure.com and perform the following steps to create an Azure Function:

1. Click on the plus button in the top-left of the page.
2. Navigate to **Compute** | **Function App** through the menu.
3. Enter a domain URL of your choice, such as `yourname-xamsnap`.
4. Choose subscription to place the services under.
5. Choose an existing **Resource Group**, or create a new one named `xamsnap`.
6. Choose a **DynamicApp Service** plan to get started. If you already have an App service plan, you can use an existing one with **Classic** mode instead.
7. Choose an existing **Storage Account** or create a new one.
8. Review your final settings and hit the **Create** button.

The management portal will display progress, and it could take a few seconds to create your Azure Function App instance.

Let's create a simple Hello World function to see things working:

1. Navigate to your Function App.
2. Click on **Quickstart**.
3. Click **Webhook + API** with C# selected then hit **Create this function**.
4. The Azure Portal will give you a quick tour, which you can skip if desired.
5. Scroll down to the bottom and click **Run** to see your Azure Function in action.

When completed, you should see output in the log window and a successful HTTP request with the output of `Hello Azure`. You should see something similar to the following screenshot:

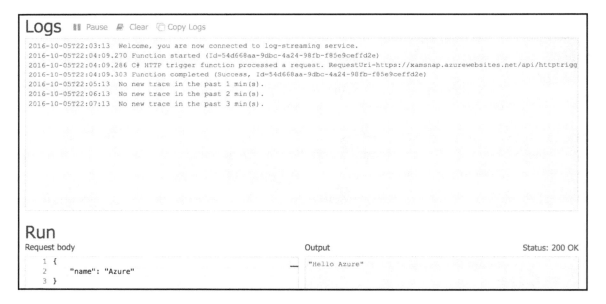

Creating and calling Azure Functions

To begin setting up our backend for XamSnap, we need to create a login function. We also need to implement the `IWebService` interface used by the rest of the application. Because of our MVVM architecture, we should be able to replace the fake service that is being used currently without changing any of the layers sitting above it.

Return to the Azure Portal, select your Function App instance, and perform the following steps:

1. Click on the **New Function** button.
2. Choose the **Empty – C#** template.
3. Enter login as the function name.
4. Click on the **Create** button.
5. Click on the **Integrate** section.
6. Add an **HTTP** trigger and output with the default settings and hit **Save**.
7. Add an **Azure Table Storage** output, change the table name to users, and hit **Save**.

Now let's write some code for our function, switch to the **Develop** section and add the following code as a starting point:

```
#r "Microsoft.WindowsAzure.Storage"

using System.Net;
using System.Text;
using Microsoft.WindowsAzure.Storage.Table;

private const string PartitionKey = "XamSnap";

public static async Task<HttpResponseMessage>
  Run(HttpRequestMessage req, CloudTable outputTable,
  TraceWriter log)
{
  dynamic data = await req.Content.ReadAsAsync<object>();
  string userName = data?.userName;
  string password = data?.password;

  if (string.IsNullOrEmpty(userName) ||
    string.IsNullOrEmpty(password))
  {
    return new HttpResponseMessage(HttpStatusCode.BadRequest);
  }
}
```

First, we added a reference to the Azure Storage SDK. This is built-in and available to Azure Functions, we will be using it later. Next, we added a few using statements and a constant. We created a static function that handles the inputs and outputs we defined earlier. `req` is the HTTP input and `outputTable` is the Azure table output. `log` is a `TraceWriter` available for debugging and logging purposes. Finally, we used built-in methods to read the POST data into `username` and `password` variables for use in our function.

Next, we need to fill in the rest of our functionality. Place this code at the bottom of the function we started:

```
//Let's hash all incoming passwords
password = Hash(password);

var operation = TableOperation.Retrieve<User>(
  PartitionKey, userName);
var result = outputTable.Execute(operation);
var existing = result.Result as User;
if (existing == null)
{
  operation = TableOperation.Insert(new User
  {
    RowKey = userName,
    PartitionKey = PartitionKey,
    PasswordHash = password,
  });
  result = outputTable.Execute(operation);

  if (result.HttpStatusCode == (int)HttpStatusCode.Created)
  {
    return new HttpResponseMessage(HttpStatusCode.OK);
  }
  else
  {
    return new HttpResponseMessage(
      (HttpStatusCode)result.HttpStatusCode);
  }
}
else if (existing.PasswordHash != password)
{
  return new HttpResponseMessage(HttpStatusCode.Unauthorized);
}
else
{
  return new HttpResponseMessage(HttpStatusCode.OK);
}
```

Let's summarize what we did in the preceding C#:

1. First, we hashed the incoming password with a function we'll add later. Note that Azure Functions have built-in authentication features that would be great for production apps. For our sample app, we are at least taking a measure to not store passwords into our database as plain text.
2. Next, we used the Azure Storage SDK to check for an existing user.
3. If there are no results, we go ahead and create a new user. The partition key and row key are concepts in Azure table storage. In most scenarios, you choose a key to partition your data, such as a state or zip code, and the row key is a unique key. For this sample, we are just using a constant value for the partition key.
4. Otherwise, we compare the hashed passwords and return a success.
5. If the passwords do not match, we return an unauthorized error code.

After this, we just need a little more code to define the `Hash` function and the `User` class:

```
private static string Hash(string password)
{
  var crypt = new System.Security.Cryptography.SHA256Managed();
  var hash = new StringBuilder();
  byte[] crypto = crypt.ComputeHash(
    Encoding.UTF8.GetBytes(password), 0,
    Encoding.UTF8.GetByteCount(password));
  foreach (byte b in crypto)
  {
    hash.Append(b.ToString("x2"));
  }
  return hash.ToString();
}

public class User : TableEntity
{
  public string PasswordHash { get; set; }
}
```

We used the built-in SHA-256 hashing algorithm found in the `System.Security` namespace. It is at least a bit more secure that the commonly broken MD5 hash. We also declared the `User` class as a table entity with one additional column containing the hash.

From here, just make sure you click on the **Save** button to apply your changes. Azure Functions also has the option of providing source control for your scripts via several source control providers. Feel free to take advantage of this feature if you want to make changes to the script in your favorite editor locally instead of the website editor. You should be able to test the function passing sample JSON as follows:

```
{
  "userName":"test",
  "password":"password"
}
```

For complete documentation for the Azure Storage SDK, make sure you check out MSDN at `https://msdn.microsoft.com/en-us/library/azure/mt347887.aspx`.

Using HttpClient in C#

With our server-side changes complete, the next step is to implement our new service in our XamSnap iOS and Android applications. Luckily, as we used an interface named `IWebService`, all we need to do is implement that interface to get it working in our application.

Now we can start setting up our service in our iOS application by performing the following steps:

1. Open the `XamSnap.Core` project that we created earlier in the book.
2. Create an `Azure` folder within the project.
3. Create a new class named `AzureWebService.cs`.
4. Make the class `public` and implement `IWebService`.
5. Right-click on `IWebService` in your code and select **Refactor | Implement Interface**.
6. A line will appear; press Enter to insert the method stubs.

When this setup is complete, your class will look something like the following:

```
public class AzureWebService : IWebService
{
  #region IWebService implementation

  public Task<User> Login(string username, string password)
  {
    throw new NotImplementedException();
  }
```

```
  // -- More methods here --

  #endregion
}
```

Next, we need to add a reference to the JSON .NET library. To do this, we will use NuGet to add the library. Right-click on the `XamSnap.Core` project and select **Add** | **Add Packages** and install Json .NET.

Now let's modify our `AzureWebService.cs` file. We will make the following changes to get started:

```
using System.Net.Http;
using System.Net.Http.Headers;
using System.Threading.Tasks;
using Newtonsoft.Json;

public class AzureWebService : IWebService
{
  private const string BaseUrl =
    "https://xamsnap.azurewebsites.net/api/";
  private const string ContentType = "application/json";
  private readonly HttpClient httpClient = new HttpClient();

  // -- Existing code here --
}
```

We defined some using statements and a few variables we will using throughout this class. Make sure you fill in the proper URL for your Azure Function App.

Next, let's write some helper methods to make calling web requests easier:

```
private async Task<HttpResponseMessage> Post(
  string url, string code, object obj)
{
  string json = JsonConvert.SerializeObject(obj);
  var content = new StringContent(json);
  content.Headers.ContentType =
    new MediaTypeHeaderValue(ContentType);

  var response = await httpClient.PostAsync(
    BaseUrl + url + "?code=" + code, content);
  response.EnsureSuccessStatusCode();
  return response;
}

private async Task<T> Post<T>(string url, string code, object obj)
{
```

```
    var response = await Post(url, code, obj);
    string json = await response.Content.ReadAsStringAsync();
    return JsonConvert.DeserializeObject<T>(json);
}}
```

Most of this code is implementing the basics for calling a RESTful endpoint in C#. First, we serialize the object to JSON and create a `StringContent` object with a header declaring that it is JSON. We format the URL with the `code` parameter, which is a simple security mechanism that is on by default for Azure Functions. Next, we call a POST request to the server and call `EnsureSuccessStatusCode` in order to throw an exception for failed requests. Lastly, we added a second method that parses the response from JSON into C# objects. Some of our Azure Functions will return data, so we will need this.

Now let's implement our first method, `Login`, in the following manner:

```
public async Task<User> Login(string userName, string password)
{
  await Post("login", "key_here", new
  {
    userName,
    password,
  });

  return new User
  {
    Name = userName,
    Password = password,
  };
}}
```

This is fairly straightforward, because of the helper methods we've already set up. We merely have to pass in our function name, its key, and the object representing the JSON we want to pass to the HTTP request. You can find the key needed under **Function URL** in the **Develop** section in the Azure Portal.

Next, open the `AppDelegate.cs` file to set up our new service and add the following code:

```
//Replace this line
ServiceContainer.Register<IWebService>(
  () => new FakeWebService());

//With this line
ServiceContainer.Register<IWebService>(
  () => new AzureWebService());
```

Now if you compile and run your application upon login, your app should successfully call your Azure Function and insert a new user into Azure Table Storage.

 If you are looking for a quick way to manage Azure Tables, Microsoft has released a free tool called Azure Storage Explorer. It is available for both Mac OS X and Windows can be found at `http://storageexplorer.com`. A second option is the **Cloud Explorer** in Visual Studio that is available if you install the Azure SDK for .NET.

Adding more Azure Functions

There are several more methods we need to implement for our `IWebService` implementation. Let's begin by adding two more Azure Functions for getting a list of a users' friends and adding a friend.

Return to the Azure Portal and perform the following steps:

1. Click on the **New Function** button.
2. Choose the **Empty – C#** template.
3. Enter `friends` as the function name.
4. Click on the **Create** button.
5. Click on the **Integrate** section.
6. Add an **HTTP** trigger and output with the default settings and hit **Save**.
7. Add an **Azure Table Storage** input, change the table name to `friends`, and hit **Save**.
8. Repeat these steps for a second function named `addfriend`, except make **Azure Table Storage** an output instead of input.

Next, let's implement the `friends` Azure Function with the following C# code:

```
#r "Microsoft.WindowsAzure.Storage"

using System.Net;
using Microsoft.WindowsAzure.Storage.Table;

public async static Task<HttpResponseMessage> Run(
    HttpRequestMessage req, IQueryable<TableEntity> inputTable,
    TraceWriter log)
{
    dynamic data = await req.Content.ReadAsAsync<object>();
    string userName = data?.userName;
    if (string.IsNullOrEmpty(userName))
```

```
  {
    return new HttpResponseMessage(HttpStatusCode.BadRequest);
  }

  var results = inputTable
    .Where(r => r.PartitionKey == userName)
    .Select(r => new { Name = r.RowKey })
    .ToList();
  return req.CreateResponse(HttpStatusCode.OK, results);
}
```

This is a bit simpler than our `login` function. Azure Functions have the option to use different types of parameters than the `CloudTable` we used earlier. When using `IQueryable` we can merely write a LINQ expression to pull out the data we need for this function: a list of friends for the specified user. We plan on storing the user's name as the `PartitionKey` and the friend's name as the `RowKey`. We then can merely return these values in the HTTP response.

Now, let's implement the `addfriend` function with the following C# code:

```
#r "Microsoft.WindowsAzure.Storage"

using System.Net;
using Microsoft.WindowsAzure.Storage.Table;

public async static Task<HttpResponseMessage> Run(
  HttpRequestMessage req, CloudTable outputTable, TraceWriter log)
{
  dynamic data = await req.Content.ReadAsAsync<object>();
  string userName = data?.userName;
  string friendName = data?.friendName;
  if (string.IsNullOrEmpty(userName) ||
    string.IsNullOrEmpty(friendName))
  {
    return new HttpResponseMessage(HttpStatusCode.BadRequest);
  }

  var operation = TableOperation.InsertOrReplace(new TableEntity
  {
    PartitionKey = userName,
    RowKey = friendName,
  });
  var result = outputTable.Execute(operation);

  return req.CreateResponse(
    (HttpStatusCode)result.HttpStatusCode);
}
```

Just as before with the `login` function, we use a `CloudTable` to add a row to an Azure Storage Table. Just as before, we handle the possibility of blank input and return the same status code the Azure Storage SDK returns.

Finally, let's modify `AzureWebService.cs`:

```
public Task<User[]> GetFriends(string userName)
{
  return Post<User[]>("friends", "key_here", new
  {
    userName
  });
}

public async Task<User> AddFriend(
  string userName, string friendName)
{
  await Post("addfriend", "key_here", new
  {
    userName,
    friendName
  });

  return new User
  {
    Name = friendName
  };
}
```

We are calling the helper methods we created earlier in the chapter to easily handle HTTP input and output to our Azure Functions. Make sure to use the proper key for each Azure Function. You may want to use a tool to insert or seed some test data into the `friends` Azure Storage table for our Azure Function to work with.

Lastly, we need to make three more Azure Functions for handling conversations and messages. Return to the Azure Portal and perform the following steps:

1. Click on the **New Function** button.
2. Choose the **Empty – C#** template.
3. Enter `conversations` as the function name.
4. Click on the **Create** button.
5. Click on the **Integrate** section.
6. Add an **HTTP** trigger and output with the default settings and hit **Save**.
7. Add an **Azure Table Storage** input, change the table name to `friends`, and hit

Save.

8. Repeat these steps for a second function named `messages` with a table name of `messages`.

9. Repeat these steps for a third function named `sendmessage`, except make **Azure Table Storage** an output instead of input.

The C# code for the `conversations` function is as follows:

```
#r "Microsoft.WindowsAzure.Storage"

using System.Net;
using Microsoft.WindowsAzure.Storage.Table;

public async static Task<HttpResponseMessage> Run(
    HttpRequestMessage req, IQueryable<Conversation> inputTable,
    TraceWriter log)
{
    dynamic data = await req.Content.ReadAsAsync<object>();
    string userName = data?.userName;
    if (string.IsNullOrEmpty(userName))
    {
        return new HttpResponseMessage(HttpStatusCode.BadRequest);
    }

    var results = inputTable
        .Where(r => r.PartitionKey == userName)
        .Select(r => new { Id = r.RowKey, UserName = r.UserName })
        .ToList();
    return req.CreateResponse(HttpStatusCode.OK, results);
}

public class Conversation : TableEntity
{
    public string UserName { get; set; }
}
```

This code is nearly identical to our `friends` function we wrote earlier. However, we need to define a `Conversation` class to add an extra column to our table beyond the default `RowKey` and `PartitionKey`.

Next, let's add the following C# code for the `messages` function:

```
#r "Microsoft.WindowsAzure.Storage"

using System.Net;
using Microsoft.WindowsAzure.Storage.Table;

public async static Task<HttpResponseMessage> Run(
  HttpRequestMessage req, IQueryable<Message> inputTable,
  TraceWriter log)
{
  dynamic data = await req.Content.ReadAsAsync<object>();
  string conversation = data?.conversation;
  if (string.IsNullOrEmpty(conversation))
  {
    return new HttpResponseMessage(HttpStatusCode.BadRequest);
  }

  var results = inputTable
    .Where(r => r.PartitionKey == conversation)
    .Select(r => new { Id = r.RowKey,
      UserName = r.UserName, Text = r.Text })
    .ToList();
  return req.CreateResponse(HttpStatusCode.OK, results);
}

public class Message : TableEntity
{
  public string UserName { get; set; }
  public string Text { get; set; }
}
```

Once again, this should be very straightforward for what we did for our `friends` and `conversations` functions.

And finally, let's add the following code for the `sendmessage` function as follows:

```
#r "Microsoft.WindowsAzure.Storage"

using System.Net;
using Microsoft.WindowsAzure.Storage.Table;

public async static Task<HttpResponseMessage> Run(
  HttpRequestMessage req, CloudTable outputTable, TraceWriter log)
{
  dynamic data = await req.Content.ReadAsAsync<object>();
  if (data == null)
    return req.CreateResponse(HttpStatusCode.BadRequest);
```

```
    var operation = TableOperation.InsertOrReplace(new Message
    {
      PartitionKey = data.Conversation,
      RowKey = data.Id,
      UserName = data.UserName,
      Text = data.Text,
    });
    var result = outputTable.Execute(operation);

    return req.CreateResponse(
      (HttpStatusCode)result.HttpStatusCode);
}

public class Message : TableEntity
{
    public string UserName { get; set; }
    public string Text { get; set; }
}
```

This function is close to what we did with `addfriend`. Later in the chapter, we will send push notifications in this function.

Before going further, let's implement the rest of our `IWebService` interface. It can be done as follows:

```
public Task<Conversation[]> GetConversations(string userName)
{
  return Post<Conversation[]>("conversations", "key_here", new
  {
    userName
  });
}

public Task<Message[]> GetMessages(string conversation)
{
  return Post<Message[]>("messages", "key_here", new
  {
    conversation
  });
}

public async Task<Message> SendMessage(Message message)
{
  message.Id = Guid.NewGuid().ToString("N");
  await Post("sendmessage", "key_here", message);
  return message;
}
```

Each method here in our client-side code is pretty simple and very similar to what we did to call the other Azure Functions. `SendMessage` is the only thing we had to do that was new: generate a unique message ID for new messages.

This completes our implementation of `IWebService`. If you run the application at this point, it will function exactly as before with the exception that the app is actually talking to a real web server. New messages will get persisted in Azure Storage Tables, and our Azure Functions will handle the custom logic that we need. Feel free to play around with our implementation; you might discover some features of Azure Functions that will work great with your own applications.

At this point, another good exercise would be to set up `AzureWebService` in our Android application. You should be able to swap out the `ServiceContainer.Register` call in your `Application` class. Everything will function exactly like on iOS. Isn't cross-platform development great?

Using the Apple Push Notification service

Implementing push notifications with Azure Notification Hubs on iOS is very simple to set up from Azure's perspective. The most complicated part is working through Apple's process of creating certificates and provisioning profiles in order to configure your iOS application. Before continuing, make sure you have a valid iOS Developer Program account, as you will not be able to send push notifications without it. If you are unfamiliar with the concept of push notifications, take a look at Apple's documentation at http://tinyurl.com/XamarinAPNS.

To send push notifications, you need to set up the following:

- An explicit App ID registered with Apple
- A provisioning profile targeting that App ID
- A certificate for your server to trigger the push notification

Apple provides both a development and production certificate, which you can use to send push notifications from your server.

Setting up your provision profile

Let's begin by navigating to `http://developer.apple.com/account`, and carry out the following steps:

1. Click on the **Identifiers** link.
2. Click on the plus button in the top-right corner of the window.
3. Enter a description, such as `XamSnap`, for the bundle ID.
4. Enter your bundle ID under the **Explicit App ID** section. This should match the bundle ID you set up in your `Info.plist` file, for example, `com.yourcompanyname.xamsnap`.
5. Under **App Services**, be sure to check **Push Notifications**.
6. Now, click on **Continue**.
7. Review your final settings and hit **Submit**.

This will create an explicit app ID similar to what we can see in the following screenshot, which we can use for sending push notifications:

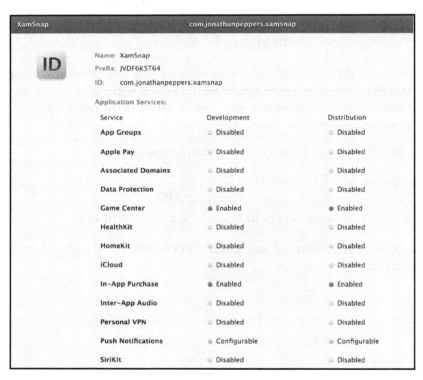

For push notifications, we have to use a profile with an explicit App ID that is not a development certificate. Now let's set up a provisioning profile:

1. Click on the **Development** link under **Provisioning Profiles** on the right-hand side.
2. Click on the plus button in the top-right corner.
3. Check **iOS App Development** and click on **Continue**.
4. Select the App ID we just created and click on **Continue**.
5. Select the developer and click on **Continue**.
6. Select the devices you will be using and click on **Continue**.
7. Enter a name for the profile and click on **Generate**.
8. Download the profile and install it, or open **XCode** and use the sync button in **Preferences | Accounts**.

When finished, you should arrive at a success web page that looks like the following:

Setting up a certificate for push notifications

Next, we perform the following steps to set up the certificate our server needs:

1. Click on the **Development** link under **Certificates** on the right-hand side.
2. Click on the plus button in the top-right corner.
3. Enable **Apple Push Notifications service SSL (Sandbox)** and click on **Continue**.
4. Select your App ID as before and click on **Continue**.

5. Create a new certificate signing request as per Apple's instructions. You may also refer to `Chapter 7`, *Deploying and Testing on Devices*, or locate the `*.certSigningRequest` file from before.

6. Next, click on **Continue**.

7. Upload the signing request file and click on **Generate**.

8. Next, click on **Download**.

9. Open the file to import the certificate into **Keychain**.

10. Locate the certificate in **Keychain**. It will be titled **Apple Development iOS Push Services** and will contain your bundle ID.

11. Right-click on the certificate and export it somewhere on your filesystem. Enter a password that you would remember.

This will create the certificate we need to send push notifications to our users from an Azure Notification Hub.

Return to the Azure Portal and perform the following steps to create an Azure Notification Hub:

1. Navigate to the resource group where your **Azure Function App** is located.

2. Click on the plus button to add a new service to the resource group.

3. Choose a **Notification Hub Name** and **Namespace** such as `xamsnap`.

4. Make sure the desired data center and resource group are selected and click on **Create**.

All that remains is to return to the Azure Portal and upload the certificate from your Azure Notification Hub. You can find this setting under **Notification Services** | **Apple (APNS)** | **Upload Certificate**, as seen in the following screenshot:

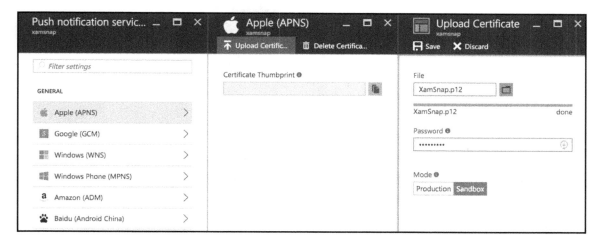

This upload concludes the configuration we need from Apple's side.

Making client-side changes for push notifications

Next, let's return to our `XamSnap.iOS` project in Xamarin Studio to make the necessary changes on the client side for push notifications. We will need to add a few new classes to our shared code to start with.

In our XamSnap PCL project, create a new interface named `INotificationService` as follows:

```
public interface INotificationService
{
  void Start(string userName);
  void SetToken(object deviceToken);
}
```

Next, we need to call `Start` after login completes. In `LoginViewModel.cs`, add the following lines after a successful login:

```
//At the top of the class
readonly INotificationService notificationService =
  ServiceContainer.Resolve<INotificationService>();

//Later, after a successful login
notificationService.Start(UserName);
```

Next, let's implement this interface in a new class in our iOS project named
`AppleNotificationService` as follows:

```
public class AppleNotificationService : INotificationService
{
  private readonly CultureInfo enUS =
    CultureInfo.CreateSpecificCulture("en-US");
  private SBNotificationHub hub;
  private string userName;
}
```

We need to define a `CultureInfo` object for use later and need two private variables for
our notification hub and the name of the currently logged in user.

Now, let's implement the `Start` method:

```
public void Start(string userName)
{
  this.userName = userName;

  var pushSettings =
    UIUserNotificationSettings.GetSettingsForTypes(
    UIUserNotificationType.Alert |
    UIUserNotificationType.Badge |
    UIUserNotificationType.Sound, null);

  UIApplication.SharedApplication
    .RegisterUserNotificationSettings(pushSettings);
}
```

We stored the user's name in a member variable and then called the native iOS APIs to set
up registration for remote notifications.

Next, we need to implement the `SetToken` method as follows:

```
public void SetToken(object deviceToken)
{
    if (hub == null)
    {
        hub = new SBNotificationHub("yourconnection", "xamsnap");
    }

    string template = "{"aps": {"alert": "$(message)"}}";
    var tags = new NSSet(userName);
    hub.RegisterTemplateAsync((NSData)deviceToken, "iOS",
      template, DateTime.Now.AddDays(90).ToString(enUS), tags,
      errorCallback =>
      {
```

```
        if (errorCallback != null)
          Console.WriteLine("Push Error: " + errorCallback);
      });
  }}
```

First, we created a new notification hub if needed. Make sure to replace `yourconnection` with a real connection string that only has **Listen** access. This can be found in the Azure Portal under **Settings | Access Policies | DefaultListenSharedAccessSignature**. Following that, we declared an iOS template that takes uses the `message` variable in the proper format for iOS push notifications. This is a feature of notification hubs that enabled cross-platform push notifications. Finally, we registered the device token with the notification hub, logging any errors that might occur.

Next, we need to make a few iOS-specific changes to `AppDelegate.cs`:

```
public override void DidRegisterUserNotificationSettings(
  UIApplication application,
  UIUserNotificationSettings notificationSettings)
{
  application.RegisterForRemoteNotifications();
}

public override void RegisteredForRemoteNotifications(
  UIApplication application, NSData deviceToken)
{
  var notificationService =
    ServiceContainer.Resolve<INotificationService>();
  notificationService.SetToken(deviceToken);
}

public override void FailedToRegisterForRemoteNotifications(
  UIApplication application, NSError error)
{
  Console.WriteLine("Push Error: " + error.LocalizedDescription);
}
```

We implemented a couple of important methods in the preceding code snippet. `DidRegisterUserNotificationSettings` is a callback for when the user accepts the iOS permission popup. `RegisteredForRemoteNotifications` will occur when Apple successfully returns a device token from its servers. We pass the device token through the `INotificationService` to the Azure Notification Hub. We also implemented `FailedToRegisterForRemoteNotifications` just to report any errors that might occur throughout the process.

Finally, we need to add a small modification to register our `INotificationService` implementation:

```
ServiceContainer.Register<INotificationService>(
  () => new AppleNotificationService());
```

Sending push notifications from the server-side

Since we have successfully configured iOS for push notifications, it is now time to actually send them from our `sendmessage` Azure Function. Azure Functions support notification hubs out of the box, but at the time of writing it was not possible to use them as an output and specify a tag targeting a specific user. Luckily, Azure Functions are just C# code, so we can easily leverage the Azure Notification Hub SDK to manually send push notifications from code. Let's switch to the Azure Portal and make the remaining changes on the server side.

First, let's add a few statements at the top to include the Azure Notification Hub SDK:

```
#r "Microsoft.Azure.NotificationHubs"
using Microsoft.Azure.NotificationHubs;
```

Next, let's add a quick method for sending push notifications:

```
private async static Task SendPush(
  string userName, string message)
{
  var dictionary = new Dictionary<string, string>();
  dictionary["message"] = userName + ": " + message;

  var hub = NotificationHubClient
    .CreateClientFromConnectionString("yourconnection "xamsnap");
  await hub.SendTemplateNotificationAsync(dictionary, userName);
}
```

Make sure to replace `yourconnection` with a valid connection string with both **Send** and **Listen** permissions. By default, you can use the one named **DefaultFullSharedAccessSignature** in the Azure Portal.

Lastly, we need to actually send the push notification when the Azure Function is invoked:

```
//Place this right before returning the HTTP response
await SendPush((string)data.UserName, (string)data.Text);
```

To test push notifications, deploy the application and log in with the secondary user. After logging in, you can just background the app with the home button. Next, log in with the primary user on your iOS simulator and send a message. You should receive a push notification, as shown in the following screenshot:

> If you are having some trouble getting things working, try sending test notifications from the Azure Portal under your notification hub and then **TroubleShooting** | **Test Send**. You can send test notifications with the native format or the custom template format we use in this chapter.

Implementing Google Cloud Messaging

Since we have already set up everything we need in the shared code and on Azure, setting up push notifications for Android will be a lot less work at this point of time. To continue, you will need a Google account with a verified e-mail address; however, I would recommend using an account registered with **Google Play**, if you have one. You can refer to the full documentation on **Google Cloud Messaging** (**GCM**) at https://developers.google.com/cloud-messaging/.

Note that Google Cloud Messaging requires that Google APIs be installed on the Android device and that the Android OS be at least Version 2.2.

Begin by navigating to http://cloud.google.com/console, then and perform the following steps:

1. Click on the **Create Project** button.
2. Enter an appropriate project name, such as XamSnap.
3. Agree to the **Terms of Service**.
4. Click on the **Create** button.
5. When creating your first project, you may have to verify the mobile number associated with your account.
6. Note the **Project Number** field on the **Overview** page. We will need this number later.

The following screenshot shows our project widget on the **Dashboard** tab:

Now we can continue with our setup as follows:

1. Click on the **Use Google APIs** widget.
2. Click on **Library** and search for **Google Cloud Messaging for Android**.
3. Click on the **Enable** button at the top to enable the service. You may have to accept another agreement.
4. Click on **Go to Credentials** that will appear in a warning tip at the top.
5. Click on the **What credentials do I need?** button.
6. Click on **Restrict Key**, choose **IP Addresses**, and enter **0.0.0.0/0**.
7. Copy the key to your clipboard for later and click **Save.**
8. Switch to the Azure Portal and navigate to the **Notification Services | Google (GCM)** section in your Azure Notification Hub instance.

9. Paste the API key in the **API Key** field and click on **Save**. Note that the first time, it may take the Google Console up to five minutes for the key to be valid.

This completes our set up on Azure's side. We will need to get a couple open-source libraries for Xamarin.Android apps. First, install **Xamarin.Azure.NotificationHubs.Android** from NuGet, and then install **Google Cloud Messaging Client** from the Xamarin Component store.

Next, create a new class called `Constants.cs` as follows:

```
public static class Constants
{
    public const string ProjectId = "yourprojectid";
    public const string ConnectionString = "yourconnectionstring";
    public const string HubName = "xamsnap";
}
```

Fill out the `ProjectId` value with the project number found earlier on the **Overview** page of your Google Cloud Console. `ConnectionString` and `HubName` should be the exact same as what was entered for iOS.

Next, we need to set up some permissions to support push notifications in our application. Above the namespace declaration in this file, add the following:

```
[assembly: Permission (Name =
  "@PACKAGE_NAME@.permission.C2D_MESSAGE")]
[assembly: UsesPermission (Name =
  "@PACKAGE_NAME@.permission.C2D_MESSAGE")]
[assembly: UsesPermission (Name =
  "com.google.android.c2dm.permission.RECEIVE")]
[assembly: UsesPermission (
  Name = "android.permission.GET_ACCOUNTS")]
[assembly: UsesPermission (
  Name = "android.permission.WAKE_LOCK")]
```

You could also make these changes in our `AndroidManifest.xml` file; however, using C# attributes can be better since it gives the ability to use code completion while typing.

Next, create another new class named `PushBroadcastReceiver.cs` as follows:

```
[BroadcastReceiver (Permission =
  Gcm.Client.Constants.PERMISSION_GCM_INTENTS)]
[IntentFilter (new string[] {
  Gcm.Client.Constants.INTENT_FROM_GCM_MESSAGE },
  Categories = new string[] { "@PACKAGE_NAME@" })]
[IntentFilter (new string[] {
  Gcm.Client.Constants.INTENT_FROM_GCM_REGISTRATION_CALLBACK },
```

```
  Categories = new string[] { "@PACKAGE_NAME@" })]
[IntentFilter(new string[] {
  Gcm.Client.Constants.INTENT_FROM_GCM_LIBRARY_RETRY },
  Categories = new string[] { "@PACKAGE_NAME@" })]
public class PushBroadcastReceiver :
  GcmBroadcastReceiverBase<PushHandlerService>
{ }
```

The `PushBroadcastReceiver.cs` class sets up `BroadcastReceiver`, which is Android's native way for different applications to talk with one another. For more information on the topic, checkout the Android documentation on the subject at http://developer.android.com/reference/android/content/BroadcastReceiver.html.

Next, create one last class named `PushHandlerService.cs` as follows:

```
[Service]
public class PushHandlerService : GcmServiceBase
{
  public PushHandlerService() : base (PushConstants.ProjectNumber)
  { }
}
```

Now, right-click on `GcmServiceBase` and choose **Refactor | Implement abstract members**. Next, let's implement each member one by one:

```
protected async override void OnRegistered(
  Context context, string registrationId)
{
  var notificationService =
    ServiceContainer.Resolve<INotificationService>();
  notificationService.SetToken(registrationId);
}
```

This preceding code is very similar to what we did on iOS. We merely have to send the `registrationId` value to `INotificationService`.

Next, we have to write the following code when the message is received:

```
protected override void OnMessage(
  Context context, Intent intent)
{
  string message = intent.Extras.GetString("message");
  if (!string.IsNullOrEmpty(message))
  {
    var notificationManager = (NotificationManager)
      GetSystemService(Context.NotificationService);
```

```
    var notification = new NotificationCompat.Builder(this)
      .SetContentIntent(
        PendingIntent.GetActivity(this, 0,
          new Intent(this, typeof(LoginActivity)), 0))
      .SetSmallIcon(Android.Resource.Drawable.SymActionEmail)
      .SetAutoCancel(true)
      .SetContentTitle("XamSnap")
      .SetContentText(message)
      .Build();
    notificationManager.Notify(1, notification);
  }
}
```

This code will actually pull out the values from the notification and display them in the notification center of the Android device. We used the built-in resource for `SymActionEmail` to display an e-mail icon in the notification.

Next, we just need to implement two more abstract methods. For now, let's just use `Console.WriteLine` to report these events, as follows:

```
protected override void OnUnRegistered(
  Context context, string registrationId)
{
  Console.WriteLine("GCM unregistered!");
}

protected override void OnError (
  Context context, string errorId)
{
  Console.WriteLine("GCM error: " + errorId);
}
```

Down the road, you should consider removing registrations from Azure when `OnUnRegistered` is called. Occasionally, a user's `registrationId` will change, so this is the place where your application is notified of this.

Next, we need to implement `INotificationService` for Android. Begin by creating a new file named `GoogleNotificationService.cs` and add the following code:

```
public class GoogleNotificationService : INotificationService
{
  readonly Context context;
  NotificationHub hub;
  string userName;

  public GoogleNotificationService(Context context)
  {
```

```
        this.context = context;
    }

    public void SetToken(object deviceToken)
    {
        hub = new NotificationHub(
            Constants.HubName, Constants.ConnectionString, context);
        try
        {
            string template = "{"data":{"message":"$(message)"}}";
            hub.RegisterTemplate((string)deviceToken,
                "Android", template, userName);
        }
        catch (Exception exc)
        {
            Console.WriteLine("RegisterTemplate Error: " + exc.Message);
        }
    }

    public void Start(string userName)
    {
        this.userName = userName;
        GcmClient.CheckDevice(context);
        GcmClient.CheckManifest(context);
        GcmClient.Register(context, Constants.ProjectId);
    }
}
```

Next, open `Application.cs` and add the following line to register our new service:

```
ServiceContainer.Register<INotificationService>(
    () => new GoogleNotificationService(this));
```

Now if you repeat the steps for testing push notifications on iOS, you should be able to send a push notification to our Android app. Even better, you should be able to send push notifications across platforms, since an iOS user could send a message to an Android user:

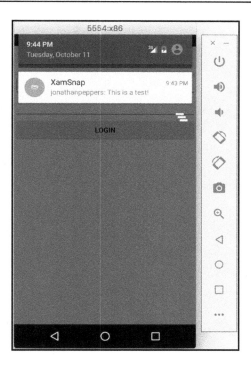

Summary

In this chapter, we went over what Windows Azure provides: Infrastructure as a Service and Platform as a Service. We set up a free Windows Azure account and set up an Azure Function App instance. We implemented the client-side code for making requests against our Azure Functions. Lastly, we implemented push notifications for iOS using Azure Notification Hubs to consolidate messages going to iOS devices via the Apple Push Notification service and Android via Google Cloud Messaging.

Using Azure Functions, we were able to get by without writing too much server-side code. In the next chapter, we'll explore how to use third-party libraries with Xamarin. This includes everything from the Xamarin Component Store to using native Objective-C or Java libraries.

10
Third-Party Libraries

Xamarin supports a subset of the .NET framework, but for the most part includes all the standard APIs you would expect in the .NET base class libraries. Because of this, a large portion of C# open-source libraries can be used directly in Xamarin projects. Additionally, if an open source project doesn't have a Xamarin or portable class library version, porting the code to be used in a Xamarin project can often be very straightforward. Xamarin also supports calling native Objective-C and Java libraries, so we will explore these as additional means of reusing existing code.

In this chapter, we will cover the following:

- The Xamarin Component Store
- Porting existing C# libraries
- Objective-C bindings
- Java bindings

The Xamarin Component Store

The primary and obvious way to add third-party components to your project is via the Xamarin Component Store. The Component Store is fairly similar to the *NuGet package manager* that all C# developers are familiar with, except that the Component Store also contains premium components that are not free. All Xamarin components are also required to include full sample projects and a Getting Started guide, while NuGet does not inherently provide documentation in its packages.

All `Xamarin.iOS` and `Xamarin.Android` projects come with a `Components` folder. To get started, simply right-click on the folder, and select **Get More Components** to launch the store dialog, shown in the following screenshot:

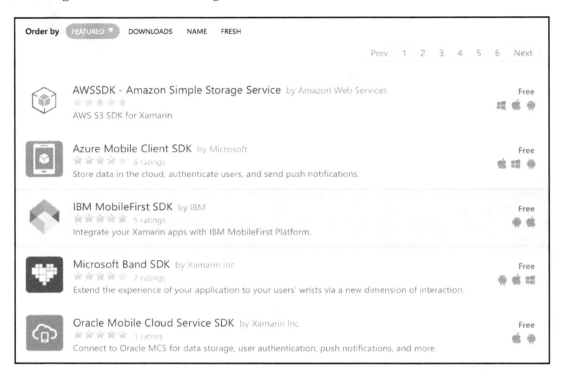

At the time of writing this book, there are well over 200 components available to enhance your iOS and Android applications. This is a great place to find the most common components to use within your Xamarin applications. Each component is complete with artwork, possibly a demonstration video, reviews, and other information you would need before purchasing a premium component.

The most well-known and useful components are as follows:

- **Json.NET**: This is the de facto standard for parsing and serializing JSON with C#
- **RestSharp**: This is a commonly used simple REST client for .NET
- **SQLite.NET**: This is a simple **Object Relational Mapping (ORM)** for working with local SQLite databases in your mobile applications
- **Facebook SDK**: This is the standard SDK provided by Facebook for integrating its services into your apps

- **Xamarin.Mobile**: This is a cross-platform library for accessing your device's contacts, GPS, photo library, and camera with a common API
- **ZXing.Net.Mobile**: A .NET version of the popular barcode-scanning library, **ZXing** (**Zebra Crossing**).

Notice that some of these libraries are native Java or Objective-C libraries, while some are plain C#. Xamarin is built from the ground up to support calling native libraries, so the Component Store offers many of the common libraries that Objective-C or Java developers would leverage when developing mobile applications.

You can also submit your own components to the Component Store. If you have a useful open source project or just want to earn a little extra cash, creating a component is simple. We won't be covering it in this book, but navigate to http://components.xamarin.com/submit for full documentation on the subject, as shown in the following screenshot:

Porting existing C# libraries

Even though Xamarin is becoming a popular platform, many open-source .NET libraries are simply not up to speed with supporting `Xamarin.iOS` and `Xamarin.Android`. But in these cases, you are definitely not out of luck. Often, if there is a Silverlight or Windows Phone version of the library, you can simply create an iOS or Android class library and add the files with no code changes.

To illustrate this process, let's port an open source project that doesn't have Xamarin or portable class library support. I have selected a dependency injection library called **Ninject**, due to its usefulness and relationship to ninjas. Find out more about the library at http://www.ninject.org/.

Let's begin setting up the library to work with Xamarin projects as follows:

1. First, download the source code for Ninject from https://github.com/ninject/ninject.
2. Create a new solution with an **iOS Class Library** project named `Ninject.iOS`.
3. Link in all the files from the `Ninject` main project. Make sure you use the **Add Existing Folder** dialog to speed up this process.

 If you aren't familiar with GitHub, I recommend downloading GitHub Desktop, a nice client app for either Windows or OS X found at `https://d esktop.github.com/`.

Now try to build the `Ninject.iOS` project; you will get several compiler errors in a file named `DynamicMethodFactory.cs`, as shown in the following screenshot:

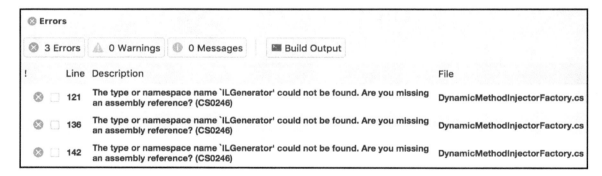

Open `DynamicMethodInjectorFactory.cs` and notice the following code at the top of the file:

```
#if !NO_LCG
namespace Ninject.Injection
{
    using System;
    using System.Reflection;
    using System.Reflection.Emit;
    using Ninject.Components;
```

```
/// *** File contents here ***

#endif
```

It is not possible to use `System.Reflection.Emit` on iOS due to Apple's platform restrictions. Luckily, the library writers have created a preprocessor directive called `NO_LCG` (which stands for **Lightweight Code Generation**) to allow the library to run on platforms that do not support `System.Reflection.Emit`.

To fix our iOS project, follow these steps:

1. Open the project options and navigate to the **Build | Compiler** section.
2. Add `NO_LCG` to the **Define Symbols** field for both **Debug** and **Release** in the **Configuration** dropdown.
3. Click on **OK** to save your changes.

If you compile the project now, it will be completed successfully and a `Ninject.iOS.dll` file will be created, which you can reference from any `Xamarin.iOS` project. You can also reference the `Ninject.iOS` project directly instead of using the `*.dll` file.

At this point, you may wish to repeat the process to create a `Xamarin.Android` class library project. Luckily, `Xamarin.Android` supports `System.Reflection.Emit`, so you can skip adding the additional preprocessor directive if you wish.

Objective-C bindings

Xamarin has developed a sophisticated system for calling native Objective-C libraries from C# in iOS projects. The core of `Xamarin.iOS` uses this same technology to call native Apple APIs in **UIKit**, **CoreGraphics**, and other iOS frameworks. Developers can create iOS binding projects to expose Objective-C classes and methods to C# using simple interfaces and attributes.

To aid in creating Objective-C bindings, Xamarin has created a small tool named **Objective Sharpie** that can process Objective-C header files for you and export the valid C# definitions to add to a binding project. This tool is a great starting point for most bindings and will get about 75% of your binding project working in most cases. You will want to hand-edit and fine-tune things to be more C#-friendly most of the time.

Note that iOS binding projects can be created in Visual Studio; however, Objective Sharpie is a command-line tool for OS X. It leverages tooling included with Xcode, so iOS binding development is best accomplished on Mac OS X.

As an example, we will write a binding for the Google Analytics library for iOS. It is a simple and useful library that can track user activities in your iOS or Android applications. At the time of writing, the version of the Google Analytics SDK is 3.17, so some of these instructions may change as new versions are released.

Download and install Objective Sharpie from `https://developer.xamarin.com/guides/cross-platform/macios/binding/objective-sharpie/` and perform the following steps:

1. Download the latest Google Analytics SDK for iOS available at https://tinyurl.com/GoogleAnalyticsForiOS.
2. Create a new **iOS | Bindings Library** project named `GoogleAnalytics.iOS`.
3. Extract the contents of the zip file from step 1 and move the `GoogleAnalytics` folder into the same directory as the bindings project.
4. Open **Terminal** and navigate to the same directory as the new project.
5. Run **Objective Sharpie** with the following commands:

```
sharpie bind --output=. --namespace=GoogleAnalytics.iOS
  --sdk=iphoneos10.0 ./GoogleAnalytics/Library/*.h
mv -f ApiDefinitions.cs ApiDefinition.cs
mv -f StructsAndEnums.cs Structs.cs
```

Objective Sharpie will output two files: `ApiDefinitions.cs` and `Structs.cs`. The second two commands will copy the files over the top of the default files from the **Bindings Library** project template created.

Note that at the time of writing, the iOS 10 SDK is used in the preceding command. To discover what you need to put for the `--sdk` option, run `sharpie xcode --sdks` and you will see the value printed in the output.

Now, if you return to your binding project, you'll notice that Objective Sharpie has generated an interface definition for every class discovered in the header files of the library. It has also generated many `enum` values that the library uses and changed casing and naming conventions to follow C# more closely where possible.

As you read through the binding, you'll notice several C# attributes that define different aspects about the Objective-C library, such as the following:

- `BaseType`: This declares an interface as an Objective-C class. The base class (also called superclass) is passed in to the attribute. If it has no base class, `NSObject` should be used.
- `Export`: This declares a method or property on an Objective-C class. A string that maps the Objective-C name to the C# name is passed in. Objective-C method names are generally in the following form:
  `myMethod:someParam:someOtherParam`.
- `Static`: This marks a method or property as `static` in C#.
- `Bind`: This is used on properties to map a getter or setter to a different Objective-C method. Objective-C properties can rename a getter or setter for a property.
- `NullAllowed`: This allows `null` to be passed to a method or property. By default, an exception is thrown if this occurs.
- `Field`: This declares an Objective-C field that is exposed as a public variable in C#.
- `Model`: This identifies a class to `Xamarin.iOS` to have methods that can be optionally overridden. This is generally used on Objective-C delegates.
- `Internal`: This flags the generated member with the C# internal keyword. It can be used to hide certain members that you don't want to expose to the outside world.
- `Abstract`: This identifies an Objective-C method as required, which goes hand in hand with `Model`. In C#, it will generate an abstract method.

The only other rule to know is how to define constructors. Xamarin had to invent a convention for this, since C# interfaces do not support constructors.

To define a constructor besides the default one, use the following code:

```
[Export("initWithFrame:")]
IntPtr Constructor(RectangleF frame);
```

This would define a constructor on the class that takes in `RectangleF` as a parameter. The method name, `Constructor`, and the return type, `IntPtr`, signal the Xamarin compiler to generate a constructor.

Now, let's return to our binding project to finish setting everything up. If you compile the project at this point, you'll get a few compiler errors. Let's fix them one by one, as follows:

1. Add `libGoogleAnalyticsServices.a` and `libAdIdAccess.a` from the Google Analytics download as **Native References**.
2. Change the base type of the enums `GAILogLevel` and `GAIDispatchResult` found in `Structs.cs` to `ulong`.
3. Remove duplicate declarations of `[Static]` from the `Constants` class found in `ApiDefinitions.cs`.
4. Remove all the `Verify` attributes. These are spots where Objective Sharpie was unsure of the operation it performed. In our example, all of them are fine, so it is safe to remove them.

At this point, if you tried to use the library in an iOS project you would get an error such as the following:

```
Error MT5210: Native linking failed, undefined symbol:
    _FooBar. Please verify that all the necessary frameworks
    have been referenced and native libraries are properly
    linked in.
```

We need to define the other frameworks and libraries that the Objective-C library uses. This is very similar to how references work in C#. If we review the Google Analytics documentation, it says that you must add `CoreData`, `SystemConfiguration`, and `libsqlite3.dylib`.

Right-click on the Native reference to `libGoogleAnalyticsServices`, choose **Properties**, and make the following changes:

1. Set `Frameworks` to `CoreData SystemConfiguration`.
2. Set `Linker Flags` to `-lsqlite3`.

Native Objective-C libraries reference other libraries with one of the following options:

- **Frameworks**: Add them to the `Frameworks` value on the `LinkWith` attribute, delimited by spaces.
- **Weak Frameworks**: Add them to the `WeakFrameworks` property on the `LinkWith` attribute in the same manner. Weak frameworks are libraries that can be ignored if they are not found. In this case, `AdSupport` was added in iOS 6; however, this library will still work on older versions of iOS.

- **Dynamic Libraries**: Libraries such as `libz.dylib` can be declared in `LinkerFlags`. Generally, you drop the `.dylib` extension and replace `lib` with `-l`.

After these changes are implemented, you will be able to successfully use the library from iOS projects. For complete documentation on Objective-C bindings, visit the Xamarin documentation site at https://developer.xamarin.com/guides/ios/.

Java bindings

In the same manner as iOS, Xamarin has provided full support for calling into Java libraries from C# with `Xamarin.Android`. The native Android SDKs function in this way and developers can leverage the `Android Java Bindings` project to take advantage of other native Java libraries in C#. The main difference here is that not a lot has to be done by hand in comparison to Objective-C bindings. The Java syntax is very similar to that of C#, so many mappings are exactly one-to-one. In addition, Java has metadata information included with its libraries, which Xamarin uses to automatically generate the C# code required for calling into Java.

As an example, let's make a binding for the Android version of the Google Analytics SDK. Before we begin, download the SDK at `https://developers.google.com/analytics/devg uides/collection/android/v3/`. At the time of writing, Google Analytics is being migrated to Google Play Services, but we will use this Java library as an exercise for creating Java bindings to be consumed by C#.

Let's begin creating a Java binding as follows:

1. Start a new `Android | Library | Bindings Library` project in Xamarin Studio. You may use the same solution as we did for iOS if you wish.
2. Name the project `GoogleAnalytics.Droid`.
3. Add `libGoogleAnalyticsServices.jar` from the Android SDK to the project under the `Jars` folder.
4. Build the project. You will get a few errors, which we'll address in a moment.

Most of the time you spend working on Java bindings will be to fix small issues that prevent the generated C# code from compiling. But don't fret; a lot of libraries will work on the first try without having to make any changes at all. Generally, the larger the Java library is, the more work you have to do to get it working with C#.

Note that if you get no errors upon first compile, but many warnings saying something to the effect of `unsupported major.minor version 52.0`, then you need to install a newer version of the Java JDK. Download JDK 1.8 from `http://tinyurl.com/XamarinJDK8`, and point Xamarin Studio or Visual Studio to the newer version of the JDK in settings.

The following are the types of issue you may run into:

- **Java obfuscation**: If the library is run through an obfuscation tool such as **ProGuard**, the class and method names may not be valid C# names.
- **Covariant return types**: Java has different rules than C# does for return types in overridden methods in subclasses. For this reason, you may need to modify the return type for the generated C# code to compile.
- **Visibility**: The rules that Java has for accessibility are different from those of C#; the visibility of methods in subclasses can be changed. Sometimes you will have to change the visibility in C# to get it to compile.
- **Naming collisions**: Sometimes, the C# code generator can get things a bit wrong and generate two members or classes with the same name.
- **Java generics**: The generic classes in Java can often cause issues in C#.

Using XPath in Java bindings

So, before we get started on solving these issues in our Java binding, let's first clean up the namespaces in the project. Java namespaces are in the form `com.mycompany.mylibrary` by default, so let's change the definition to match C# more closely. In the `Transforms` directory of the project, open `Metadata.xml` and add the following XML tag inside the root metadata node:

```
<attr path="/api/package[@name='com.google.analytics.tracking
    .android']" name="managedName">GoogleAnalytics.Tracking</attr>
```

The `attr` node tells the Xamarin compiler what needs to be replaced, in the Java definition, with another value. In this case, we are replacing `managedName` of the package with `GoogleAnalytics.Tracking` because it will make much more sense in C#. The path value may look a bit strange, which is because it is using an XML matching query language named **XPath**. In general, just think of it as a pattern matching query for XML. For full documentation on XPath syntax, check out some of the many resources online, such as `http://w3schools.com/xpath`.

You may be asking yourself at this point, what is the XPath expression matching against? Return to Xamarin Studio and right-click on the solution at the top. Click on **Display Options** | **Show All Files**. Open api.xml under the Debug folder in obj. This is the Java definition file that describes all types and methods within the Java library. You may notice that the XML here directly correlates to the XPath expressions we'll be writing.

For our next step, let's remove all the packages (or namespaces) we don't plan on using in this library. This is generally a good idea for large libraries, since you don't want to waste time fixing issues with parts of the library you won't even be calling from C#.

Add the following declarations in Metadata.xml:

```
<remove-node path="/api/package[@name='com.google.analytics
    .containertag.common']" />
<remove-node path="/api/package[@name='com.google.analytics
    .containertag.proto']" />
<remove-node path="/api/package[@name='com.google.analytics
    .midtier.proto.containertag']" />
<remove-node path="/api/package[@name='com.google.android
    .gms.analytics.internal']" />
<remove-node path="/api/package[@name='com.google.android
    .gms.common.util']" />
<remove-node
    path="/api/package[@name='com.google.tagmanager']" />
<remove-node
    path="/api/package[@name='com.google.tagmanager.proto']" />
<remove-node
    path="/api/package[@name='com.google.tagmanager.protobuf.nano']" />
```

Note that removing these namespaces does not actually remove the compiled Java code from your binding. It merely prevents the binding project from generating the C# code to use classes in this namespace.

Now when you build the library, we can start resolving issues. The first error you will receive will be something like the following:

```
GoogleAnalytics.Tracking.GoogleAnalytics.cs(74,74):
    Error CS0234: The type or namespace name `TrackerHandler'
    does not exist in the namespace `GoogleAnalytics.Tracking'.
    Are you missing an assembly reference?
```

If we locate `TrackerHandler` within the `api.xml` file, we'll see the following class declaration:

```
<class
    abstract="true" deprecated="not deprecated"
    extends="java.lang.Object"
    extends-generic-aware="java.lang.Object"
    final="false" name="TrackerHandler"
    static="false" visibility=""/>
```

So, can you spot the problem? We need to fill out the `visibility` XML attribute, which for some reason is blank. Add the following line to `Metadata.xml`:

```
<attr
  path="/api/package[@name='com.google.analytics
  .tracking.android']/class[@name='TrackerHandler']"
  name="visibility">public</attr>
```

This XPath expression will locate the `TrackerHandler` class inside the `com.google.analytics.tracking.android` package and change `visibility` to `public`.

If you build the project now, it will complete successfully with a few warnings. In Java binding projects, it is a good idea to fix warnings where possible, since they generally indicate that a class or method is being omitted from the binding. Notice the following warning:

```
GoogleAnalytics.Droid: Warning BG8102:
    Class GoogleAnalytics.Tracking.CampaignTrackingService has
    unknown base type android.app.IntentService (BG8102)
    (GoogleAnalytics.Droid)
```

To fix this issue, locate the type definition for `CampaignTrackingService` in `api.xml`, which would be as follows:

```
<class
    abstract="false" deprecated="not deprecated"
    extends="android.app.IntentService"
    extends-generic-aware="android.app.IntentService"
    final="false" name="CampaignTrackingService"
    static="false" visibility="public">
```

The way to fix the issue here is to change the base class to the `Xamarin.Android` definition for `IntentService`. Add the following code to `Metadata.xml`:

```
<attr
    path="/api/package[@name='com.google.analytics
    .tracking.android']/class[@name='CampaignTrackingService']"
    name="extends">mono.android.app.IntentService</attr>
```

This changes the `extends` attribute to use the `IntentService` found in `Mono.Android.dll`. I located the Java name for this class by opening `Mono.Android.dll` in Xamarin Studio's **Assembly Browser** and looking at the `Register` attribute, as shown in the following screenshot:

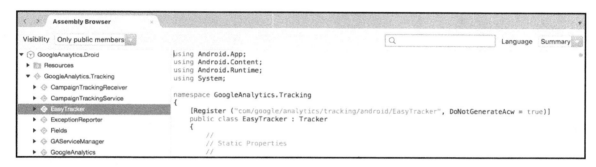

To inspect `*.dll` files in Xamarin Studio, you merely have to open them. You can also double-click on any assembly in the `References` folder in your project.

If you build the binding project now, we're left with one last error, as follows:

```
GoogleAnalytics.Tracking.CampaignTrackingService.cs(24,24):
    Error CS0507:
    `CampaignTrackingService.OnHandleIntent(Intent)':
    cannot change access modifiers when overriding `protected'
    inherited member
    `IntentService.OnHandleIntent(Android.Content.Intent)'
    (CS0507) (GoogleAnalytics.Droid)
```

If you navigate to the `api.xml` file, you can see the definition for `OnHandleIntent` as follows:

```
<method
    abstract="false" deprecated="not deprecated" final="false"
    name="onHandleIntent" native="false" return="void"
    static="false" synchronized="false" visibility="public">
```

We can see here that the Java method for this class is `public`, but the base class is `protected`. So, the best way to fix this is to change the C# version to `protected` as well. Writing an XPath expression to match this is a bit more complicated, but luckily, Xamarin has an easy way to retrieve it. If you double-click on the error message in the **Errors** pad of Xamarin Studio, you'll see the following comment in the generated C# code:

```
// Metadata.xml XPath method reference:
   path="/api/package[@name='com.google.analytics
   .tracking.android']/class[@name='CampaignTrackingService']
   /method[@name='onHandleIntent' and count(parameter)=1 and
   parameter[1][@type='android.content.Intent']]"
```

Copy this value of `path`, and add the following to `Metadata.xml`:

```
<attr path="/api/package[@name='com.google.analytics
   .tracking.android']/class[@name='CampaignTrackingService']
   /method[@name='onHandleIntent' and count(parameter)=1 and
   parameter[1][@type='android.content.Intent']]"
   name="visibility">protected</attr>
```

Now, we can build the project and only have warnings related to `[Obsolete]` members being overridden (nothing to worry about). The library is now ready for use within your `Xamarin.Android` projects.

However, if you start working with the library, notice how the parameter names for methods are p0, p1, p2, and so on. Here are a few method definitions of the `EasyTracker` class:

```
public static EasyTracker GetInstance(Context p0);
public static void SetResourcePackageName(string p0);
public virtual void ActivityStart(Activity p0);
public virtual void ActivityStop(Activity p0);
```

You can imagine how difficult it could be to consume a Java library without knowing the proper parameter names. The reason the parameters are named this way is because the Java metadata for its libraries does not include the information to set the proper name for each parameter. So, `Xamarin.Android` does the best thing it can and autonames each parameter sequentially.

To rename the parameters in this class, we can add the following to `Metadata.xml`:

```
<attr path="/api/package[@name='com.google.analytics
   .tracking.android']/class[@name='EasyTracker']
   /method[@name='getInstance']/parameter[@name='p0']"
   name="name">context</attr>
<attr path="/api/package[@name='com.google.analytics
```

```
       .tracking.android']/class[@name='EasyTracker']
       /method[@name='setResourcePackageName']/parameter[@name='p0']"
       name="name">packageName</attr>
   <attr path="/api/package[@name='com.google.analytics
       .tracking.android']/class[@name='EasyTracker']
       /method[@name='activityStart']/parameter[@name='p0']"
       name="name">activity</attr>
   <attr path="/api/package[@name='com.google.analytics
       .tracking.android']/class[@name='EasyTracker']
       /method[@name='activityStop']/parameter[@name='p0']"
       name="name">activity</attr>
```

Upon rebuilding the binding project, this will effectively rename the parameters for these four methods in the `EasyTracker` class. At this time, I would recommend going through the classes you plan on using in your application and renaming the parameters so that it will make more sense to you. You might need to refer to the Google Analytics documentation to get the naming correct. Luckily, there is a `javadocs.zip` file included in the SDK that provides HTML references for the library.

For a full reference on implementing Java bindings, make sure to check out Xamarin's documentation site at `https://developer.xamarin.com/guides/android/`. There are certainly more complicated scenarios than what we ran into when creating a binding for the Google Analytics library.

Summary

In this chapter, we added libraries from the Xamarin Component Store to Xamarin projects and ported an existing C# library, Ninject, to both `Xamarin.iOS` and `Xamarin.Android`. Next, we installed Objective Sharpie and explored its usage for generating Objective-C bindings. Finally, we wrote a functional Objective-C binding for the Google Analytics SDK for iOS and a Java binding for the Google Analytics SDK for Android. We also wrote several XPath expressions to clean up the Java binding.

There are several available options for using existing third-party libraries from your `Xamarin.iOS` and `Xamarin.Android` applications. We looked at everything from using the Xamarin Component Store, porting existing code, and setting up Java and Objective-C libraries to be used from C#. In the next chapter, we will cover the `Xamarin.Mobile` library as a way to access a user's contacts, camera, and GPS location.

11
Xamarin.Forms

Since the beginning of Xamarin's life as a company, their motto has always been to present the native APIs on iOS and Android idiomatically to C#. This was a great strategy in the beginning, because applications built with Xamarin.iOS or Xamarin.Android were pretty much indistinguishable from native Objective-C or Java applications. Code sharing was generally limited to non-UI code, which left a potential gap to fill in the Xamarin ecosystem: a cross-platform UI abstraction. Xamarin.Forms is the solution to this problem, a cross-platform UI framework that renders native controls on each platform. `Xamarin.Forms` is a great framework for those that know C# (and XAML), but also may not want to get into the full details of using the native iOS and Android APIs.

In this chapter, we will do the following:

- Create *Hello World* in Xamarin.Forms
- Discuss the Xamarin.Forms architecture
- Use XAML with Xamarin.Forms
- Cover data binding and MVVM with Xamarin.Forms

Creating Hello World in Xamarin.Forms

To understand how a Xamarin.Forms application is put together, let's begin by creating a simple *Hello World* application.

Open Xamarin Studio and perform the following steps:

1. Create a new **Multiplatform | App | Forms App** project from the new solution dialog.
2. Name your solution something appropriate, such as `HelloForms`.

3. Make sure **Use Portable Class Library** is selected.
4. Click **Next**, then click **Create**.

Notice the three new projects that were successfully created:

- HelloForms
- HelloForms.Android
- HelloForms.iOS

In `Xamarin.Forms` applications, the bulk of your code will be shared, and each platform-specific project is just a small amount of code that starts up the Xamarin.Forms framework.

Let's examine the minimum parts of a Xamarin.Forms application:

- `App.xaml` and `App.xaml.cs` in the `HelloForms` PCL library — this class is the main starting point of the Xamarin.Forms application. A simple property, `MainPage`, is set to the first page in the application. In the default project template, `HelloFormsPage` is created with a single label that will be rendered as a `UILabel` on iOS and a `TextView` on Android.
- `MainActivity.cs` in the `HelloForms.Android` Android project — the main launcher activity of the Android application. The important parts for Xamarin.Forms here is the call to `Forms.Init(this, bundle)`, which initializes the Android-specific portion of the Xamarin.Forms framework. Next is a call to `LoadApplication(new App())`, which starts our Xamarin.Forms application.
- `AppDelegate.cs` in the `HelloForms.iOS` iOS project — very similar to Android, except iOS applications start up using a `UIApplicationDelegate` class. `Forms.Init()` will initialized the iOS-specific parts of Xamarin.Forms, and just as Android's `LoadApplication(new App())`, will start the Xamarin.Forms application.

Go ahead and run the iOS project; you should see something similar to the following screenshot:

If you run the Android project, you will get a UI very similar to the iOS one shown in the following screenshot, but using native Android controls:

Even though it's not covered in this book, Xamarin.Forms also supports Windows Phone, WinRT, and UWP applications. However, a PC running Windows and Visual Studio is required to develop for Windows platforms. If you can get a Xamarin.Forms application working on iOS and Android, then getting a Windows Phone version working should be a piece of cake.

Understanding the architecture behind Xamarin.Forms

Getting started with Xamarin.Forms is very easy, but it is always good to look behind the scenes to understand how everything is put together. In the earlier chapters of this book, we created a cross-platform application using native iOS and Android APIs directly. Certain applications are much more suited for this development approach, so understanding the difference between a Xamarin.Forms application and a *classic* Xamarin application is important when choosing what framework is best suited for your app.

Xamarin.Forms is an abstraction over the native iOS and Android APIs that you can call directly from C#. So, Xamarin.Forms is using the same APIs you would in a *classic* Xamarin application, while providing a framework that allows you to define your UIs in a cross-platform way. An abstraction layer such as this is in many ways a very good thing, because it gives you the benefit of sharing the code driving your UI as well as any backend C# code that could also have been shared in a standard Xamarin app. The main disadvantage, however, is a slight hit in performance that might make it more difficult to create a perfect, buttery-smooth experience. Xamarin.Forms gives the option of writing **renderers** and **effects** that allow you to override your UI in a platform-specific way. This gives you the ability to drop down to native controls where needed.

Have a look at the differences between a Xamarin.Forms application and a traditional Xamarin app in the following diagram:

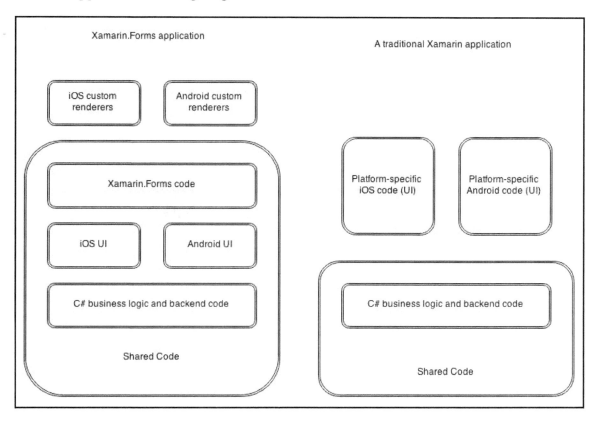

In both applications, the business logic and backend code of the application can be shared, but Xamarin.Forms gives an enormous benefit by allowing your UI code to be shared as well.

Additionally, Xamarin.Forms applications have two project templates to choose from, so let's cover each option:

- **Xamarin.Forms Shared**: Creates a shared project with all of your Xamarin.Forms code, an iOS project, and an Android project
- **Xamarin.Forms Portable**: Creates a **Portable Class Library** (**PCL**) containing all shared Xamarin.Forms code, an iOS project, and an Android project

Both options will work well for any application, in general. Shared projects are basically a collection of code files that get added automatically by another project referencing it. Using a shared project allows you to use preprocessor statements to implement platform-specific code. PCL projects, on the other hand, create a portable .NET assembly that can be used on iOS, Android, and various other platforms. PCLs can't use preprocessor statements, so you generally set up platform-specific code with interface or abstract/base classes. In most cases, I think a PCL is a better option, since it inherently encourages better programming practices. See Chapter 3, *Code Sharing between iOS and Android*, for details on the advantages and disadvantages of these two code-sharing techniques.

Using XAML in Xamarin.Forms

In addition to defining Xamarin.Forms controls from C# code, Xamarin has provided the tooling for developing your UI in **Extensible Application Markup Language (XAML)**. XAML is a declarative language that is basically a set of XML elements that map to a certain control in the Xamarin.Forms framework. Using XAML is comparable to using HTML to define the UI on a webpage, with the exception that XAML in Xamarin.Forms is creating C# objects that represent a native UI.

To understand how XAML works in Xamarin.Forms, let's create a new page with different types of Xamarin.Forms controls on it. Return to your HelloForms project from earlier, and open the HelloFormsPage.xaml file. Add the following XAML code between the <ContentPage> tags:

```
<StackLayout Orientation="Vertical" Padding="10,20,10,10">
    <Label Text="My Label" XAlign="Center" />
    <Button Text="My Button" />
    <Entry Text="My Entry" />
    <Image Source="https://www.xamarin.com/content/images/
      pages/branding/assets/xamagon.png" />
    <Switch IsToggled="true" />
    <Stepper Value="10" />
</StackLayout>
```

Go ahead and run the application on iOS; your application will look something like the following screenshot:

On Android, the application looks identical to iOS, except it is using native Android controls instead of the iOS counterparts:

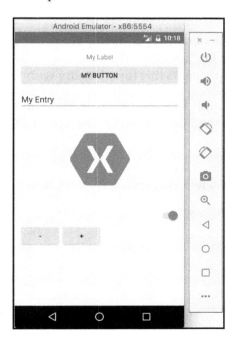

In our XAML, we created a `StackLayout` control, which is a container for other controls. It can lay out controls either vertically or horizontally one by one, as defined by the `Orientation` value. We also applied a padding of 10 around the sides and bottom, and 20 from the top to adjust for the iOS status bar. You may be familiar with this syntax for defining rectangles if you are familiar with WPF or Silverlight. Xamarin.Forms uses the same syntax of left, top, right, and bottom values, delimited by commas.

We also used several of the built-in Xamarin.Forms controls to see how they work:

1. `Label`: We used this earlier in the chapter. Used only for displaying text, this maps to a `UILabel` on iOS and a `TextView` on Android.
2. `Button`: A general purpose button that can be tapped by a user. This control maps to a `UIButton` on iOS and a `Button` on Android.
3. `Entry`: This control is a single-line text entry. It maps to a `UITextField` on iOS and an `EditText` on Android.
4. `Image`: This is a simple control for displaying an image on the screen, which maps to a `UIImage` on iOS and an `ImageView` on Android. We used the `Source` property of this control, which loads an image from a web address. Using URLs on this property is nice, but it is best for performance to include the image in your project where possible.
5. `Switch`: This is an on/off switch or toggle button. It maps to a `UISwitch` on iOS and a `Switch` on Android.
6. `Stepper`: This is a general-purpose input for entering numbers using two plus and minus buttons. On iOS, this maps to a `UIStepper`, while on Android, Xamarin.Forms implements this functionality with two buttons.

These are just some of the controls provided by Xamarin.Forms. There are also more complicated controls, such as the `ListView` and `TableView`, which you would expect for delivering mobile UIs.

Even though we used XAML in this example, you could also implement this Xamarin.Forms page from C#. Here is an example of what that would look like:

```
public class UIDemoPageFromCode : ContentPage
{
  public UIDemoPageFromCode()
  {
    var layout = new StackLayout
    {
      Orientation = StackOrientation.Vertical,
      Padding = new Thickness(10, 20, 10, 10),
    };
```

```
layout.Children.Add(new Label
{
  Text = "My Label",
  XAlign = TextAlignment.Center,
});

layout.Children.Add(new Button
{
  Text = "My Button",
});

layout.Children.Add(new Image
{
  Source = "https://www.xamarin.com/content/images/pages/
    branding/assets/xamagon.png",
});

layout.Children.Add(new Switch
{
  IsToggled = true,
});

layout.Children.Add(new Stepper
{
  Value = 10,
});

  Content = layout;
  }
}
```

So, you can see where using XAML can be a bit more readable, and is generally a bit better at declaring UIs than C#. However, using C# to define your UIs is still a viable, straightforward approach.

Using data-binding and MVVM

At this point, you should be grasping the basics of Xamarin.Forms, but are wondering how the MVVM design pattern fits into the picture. The MVVM design pattern was originally conceived for use along with XAML and the powerful data binding features XAML provides, so it is only natural that it is a perfect design pattern to be used with Xamarin.Forms.

Let's cover the basics of how data-binding and MVVM is set up with Xamarin.Forms:

1. Your Model and ViewModel layers will remain mostly unchanged from the MVVM pattern we covered earlier in the book.

2. Your ViewModels should implement the `INotifyPropertyChanged` interface, which facilitates data binding. To simplify things in Xamarin.Forms, you can use the `BindableObject` base class and call `OnPropertyChanged` when values change on your ViewModels.

3. Any `Page` or control in Xamarin.Forms has a `BindingContext`, which is the object that it is data-bound to. In general, you can set a corresponding ViewModel to each view's `BindingContext` property.

4. In XAML, you can set up a data-binding by using syntax of the form `Text="{Binding Name}"`. This example would bind the `Text` property of the control to a `Name` property of the object residing in the `BindingContext`.

5. In conjunction with data binding, events can be translated to commands using the `ICommand` interface. So, for example, the click event of a `Button` can be data-bound to a command exposed by a ViewModel. There is a built-in `Command` class in Xamarin.Forms to support this.

 Data binding can also be set up with C# code in Xamarin.Forms using the `Binding` class. However, it is generally much easier to set up bindings with XAML, since the syntax has been simplified with XAML markup extensions.

Now that we have covered the basics, let's go through step-by-step and partially convert our `XamSnap` sample application from earlier in the book to use Xamarin.Forms. For the most part, we can reuse most of the Model and ViewModel layers, although we will have to make a few minor changes to support data-binding with XAML.

Let's begin by creating a new Xamarin.Forms application backed by a PCL, named `XamSnap`:

1. First, create three folders in the `XamSnap` project named `Views`, `ViewModels`, and `Models`.

2. Add the appropriate `ViewModels` and `Models` classes from the `XamSnap` application from earlier chapters; these are found in the `XamSnap` project.

3. Build the project, just to make sure everything is saved. You will get a few compiler errors, which we will resolve shortly.

The first class we will need to edit is the `BaseViewModel` class; open it and make the following changes:

```
public class BaseViewModel : BindableObject
{
  protected readonly IWebService service =
    DependencyService.Get<IWebService>();
  protected readonly ISettings settings =
    DependencyService.Get<ISettings>();

  bool isBusy = false;

  public bool IsBusy
  {
    get { return isBusy; }
    set
    {
      isBusy = value;
      OnPropertyChanged();
    }
  }
}
```

First of all, we removed the calls to the `ServiceContainer` class, because Xamarin.Forms provides its own IoC container called the `DependencyService`. It functions very similarly to the container we built in the previous chapters, except it only has one method, `Get<T>`, and registrations are set up via an assembly attribute that we will set up shortly.

Additionally, we removed the `IsBusyChanged` event in favor of the `INotifyPropertyChanged` interface that supports data binding. Inheriting from `BindableObject` gave us the helper method, `OnPropertyChanged`, which we use to inform bindings in Xamarin.Forms that the value has changed. Notice we didn't pass a `string` containing the property name to `OnPropertyChanged`. This method is using a lesser-known feature of .NET 4.0 called `CallerMemberName`, which will automatically fill in the calling property's name at runtime.

Next, let's set up the services we need with the `DependencyService`. Open `App.xaml.cs` in the root of the PCL project and add the following two lines above the namespace declaration:

```
[assembly: Dependency(typeof(XamSnap.FakeWebService))]
[assembly: Dependency(typeof(XamSnap.FakeSettings))]
```

The `DependencyService` will automatically pick up these attributes and inspect the types we declared. Any interfaces these types implement will be returned for any future callers of `DependencyService.Get<T>`. I normally put all `Dependency` declarations in the `App.cs` file, just so they are easy to manage and in one place.

Next, let's modify `LoginViewModel` by adding a new property:

```
public Command LoginCommand { get; set; }
```

We'll use this shortly for data-binding the command of a `Button`. One last change in the view model layer is to set up `INotifyPropertyChanged` for `MessageViewModel`:

```
Conversation[] conversations;

public Conversation[] Conversations
{
  get { return conversations; }
  set
  {
    conversations = value;
    OnPropertyChanged();
  }
}
```

Likewise, you could repeat this pattern for the remaining public properties throughout the view model layer, but this is all we will need for this example. Next, let's create a new `Forms ContentPage Xaml` file named `LoginPage` in the `Views` folder. In the code-behind file, `LoginPage.xaml.cs`, we'll just need to make a few changes:

```
public partial class LoginPage : ContentPage
{
  readonly LoginViewModel loginViewModel = new LoginViewModel();


  public LoginPage()
  {
    Title = "XamSnap";
    BindingContext = loginViewModel;

    loginViewModel.LoginCommand = new Command(async () =>
    {
      try
      {
        await loginViewModel.Login();
        await Navigation.PushAsync(new ConversationsPage());
      }
      catch (Exception exc)
```

```
    {
        await DisplayAlert("Oops!", exc.Message, "Ok");
    }
    });

    InitializeComponent();
  }
}
```

We did a few important things here, including setting the `BindingContext` to our `LoginViewModel`. We set up the `LoginCommand`, which basically invokes the `Login` method and displays a message if something goes wrong. It also navigates to a new page if successful. We also set the `Title`, which will show up in the top navigation bar of the application.

Next, open `LoginPage.xaml` and we'll add the following XAML code inside `ContentPage`:

```
<StackLayout Orientation="Vertical" Padding="10,10,10,10">
    <Entry
        Placeholder="Username" Text="{Binding UserName}" />
    <Entry
        Placeholder="Password" Text="{Binding Password}"
        IsPassword="true" />
    <Button
        Text="Login" Command="{Binding LoginCommand}" />
    <ActivityIndicator
        IsVisible="{Binding IsBusy}"
        IsRunning="true" />
</StackLayout>
```

This will set up the basics of two text fields, a button, and a spinner, complete with all the bindings to make everything work. Since we set up `BindingContext` from the `LoginPage` code-behind file, all the properties are bound to `LoginViewModel`.

Next, create `ConversationsPage` as a XAML page just like before, and edit the `ConversationsPage.xaml.cs` code-behind file:

```
public partial class ConversationsPage : ContentPage
{
  readonly MessageViewModel messageViewModel =
    new MessageViewModel();

  public ConversationsPage()
```

```
{
  Title = "Conversations";
  BindingContext = messageViewModel;

  InitializeComponent();
}

protected async override void OnAppearing()
{
  try
  {
    await messageViewModel.GetConversations();
  }
  catch (Exception exc)
  {
    await DisplayAlert("Oops!", exc.Message, "Ok");
  }
}
}
```

In this case, we repeated a lot of the same steps. The exception is that we used the
`OnAppearing` method as a way to load the conversations to display on the screen.

Now let's add the following XAML code to `ConversationsPage.xaml`:

```
<ListView ItemsSource="{Binding Conversations}">
    <ListView.ItemTemplate>
        <DataTemplate>
            <TextCell Text="{Binding UserName}" />
        </DataTemplate>
    </ListView.ItemTemplate>
</ListView>
```

In this example, we used `ListView` to data-bind a list of items and display on the screen.
We defined a `DataTemplate` class, which represents a set of cells for each item in the list
that the `ItemsSource` is data-bound to. In our case, a `TextCell` displaying the `Username`
is created for each item in the `Conversations` list.

Last but not least, we must return to the `App.xaml.cs` file and modify the startup page:

```
MainPage = new NavigationPage(new LoginPage());
```

We used a `NavigationPage` here so that Xamarin.Forms can push and pop between different pages. This uses a `UINavigationController` on iOS, so you can see how the native APIs are being used on each platform.

At this point, if you compile and run the application, you will get a functional iOS and Android application that can log in and view a list of conversations:

Summary

In this chapter, we covered the basics of Xamarin.Forms and how it can be very useful for building your own cross-platform applications. Xamarin.Forms shines for certain types of apps, but can be limiting if you need to write more complicated UIs or take advantage of native drawing APIs. We discovered how to use XAML for declaring our Xamarin.Forms UIs and understood how Xamarin.Forms controls are rendered on each platform. We also dived into the concepts of data-binding and how to use the MVVM design pattern with Xamarin.Forms. Last but not least, we began porting the `XamSnap` application from earlier in the book to Xamarin.Forms, and were able to reuse a lot of our existing code.

In the next chapter, we will cover the process of submitting applications to the iOS App Store and Google Play. Getting your app into the store can be a time-consuming process, but guidance from the next chapter will give you a head start.

12
App Store Submission

Now that you have completed the development of your cross-platform application, the next obvious step is to distribute your app on Google Play and iOS App Store. Xamarin apps are distributed in exactly the same way as Java or Objective-C apps; however, it can be a bit of a pain to get your app through the process. iOS has an official approval system, which makes app store submission a lengthier process than Android. Developers might have to wait for a week or longer, depending on how many times the app is rejected. Android requires some additional steps to submit the app on Google Play compared to debugging your application, but you can still get your application submitted in just a few hours.

In this chapter, we will cover:

- The App Store Review Guidelines
- Submitting an iOS app to the App Store
- Setting up Android signing keys
- Submitting an Android app to Google Play
- Tips for being successful on app stores

Following the iOS App Store Review Guidelines

Your application's name, app icon, screenshots, and other aspects are declared on Apple's website, called iTunes Connect. Sales reports, app store rejections, contract and bank information, and app updates are all managed through the website at `http://itunesconnect.apple.com`.

The primary purpose of Apple's guidelines is to keep the iOS App Store safe and free of malware. There is certainly little to no malware found on the iOS App Store. Generally, the worst thing an iOS application could do to you is bombard you with ads. To a certain extent, the guidelines also reinforce Apple's revenue share with payments within your application. Sadly, some of Apple's guidelines controversially eliminate a competitor in a key area on iOS:

The key point here is to get your applications through the store approval process without facing App Store rejections. As long as you are not intentionally trying to break the rules, most applications will not face difficulty in getting approved. The most common rejections are related to mistakes by developers, which is a good thing, since you would not want to release an app with a critical issue to the public.

The App Store Review Guidelines are quite lengthy, so let's break it down into the most common situations you might run into. A full list of the guidelines is found at `https://developer.apple.com/app-store/review/guidelines/`.

Some general rules to note are:

- Applications that crash, have bugs, or fail critically will be rejected
- Applications that do not perform as advertised or contain hidden features will be rejected
- Applications that use non-public Apple APIs, or read/write files from prohibited locations on the filesystem will be rejected
- Apps that provide little value or that have been overdone (such as flashlight, burp, or fart apps) will be rejected
- Applications cannot use trademarked words as the app name or keywords without the permission of the trademark holder
- Applications cannot distribute copyrighted material illegally
- Apps that can simply be implemented by a mobile-friendly website, such as apps with lots of HTML content that provide no native functionality, can be rejected

These rules make sense to keep the overall quality and safety of the iOS App Store higher than it would have otherwise been. It can be difficult to get a simple app with very few features into the store due to some of these rules, so be sure that your app is useful and compelling enough for the App Store review team to allow it to be available on the store.

Some rules related to the mistakes made by developers or incorrect labeling in iTunes Connect are as follows:

- Applications or metadata that mention other mobile platforms such as Android, for example, will be rejected
- Applications that are labeled with an incorrect or inappropriate category/genre, screenshots, or icons will be rejected
- Developers must give an appropriate age rating and keywords for the application
- Support, privacy policy, and marketing URLs must be functional at the time the app is reviewed
- Developers should not declare iOS features that are not used; for example, do not declare Game Center or iCloud usage if your application does not actually use these features
- Applications that use features such as location or push notifications without the consent of the user will be rejected

These can sometimes simply be a mistake on the developer's part. Just make sure you double-check all of your application's information before that final submission to the iOS App Store.

Additionally, Apple has the following rules regarding content that can be contained within an application:

- Applications that contain objectionable content or content that may be considered rude will be rejected
- Applications that are designed to upset or disgust users will be rejected
- Applications that contain excessive imagery of violence will be rejected
- Applications that target a specific government, race, culture, or company as enemies will be rejected
- Applications with icons or screenshots that do not adhere to the 4+ age rating may be rejected

The App Store delivers apps to children and adults alike. Apple also supports an *over 17* age restriction on applications; however, this will seriously limit the number of potential users. It's best to keep applications clean and appropriate for as many ages as possible.

The next category of rules, listed as follows, are related to Apple's 70/30 revenue share from the App Store:

- Applications that link to products or software sold on a website may be rejected.
- Apps using a payment mechanism other than iOS **In-App Purchases** (**IAPs**) will be rejected.
- Applications that use IAPs for purchasing physical goods will be rejected.
- Apps can display digital content that is purchased outside the application as long as you cannot link to or purchase from within the app. All digital content purchased within the app must use IAPs.

These rules are easy to follow, as long as you are not trying to circumvent Apple's revenue share in the App Store. Always use IAPs for unlocking digital content within your applications.

Last but not least, here are some general tips related to App Store rejections:

- If your application requires a username and password, be sure to include credentials under the **Demo Account Information** section for the app review team to use.
- If your application contains IAPs or other features that the app review team must explicitly test, be sure to include instructions in **Review Notes** to reach the appropriate screen in your application.

- Schedule ahead! Don't let your product's app rejection ruin a deadline; plan at least a few weeks into your schedule for App Store approval. Another option is to submit a beta build ahead of time for approval, with the release date set in the future. You can upload a final build closer to the release date.
- When in doubt, be as descriptive as possible in the **Review Notes** section of iTunes Connect.

If your application does get rejected, most of the time there is an easy resolution. Apple's review team will explicitly reference the guidelines if a rule is broken, and will include the relevant crash logs and screenshots. If you can correct an issue without submitting a new build, you can respond to the app review team using the **Resolution Center** option in the iTunes Connect website. If you upload a new build, this will put your application at the end of the queue to be reviewed.

There are certainly more in-depth and specific rules for features in iOS, so make sure you have a look at the complete set of guidelines if you are thinking about doing something creative or out of the box with an iOS feature. As always, if you are unsure about a specific guideline, it is best to seek professional, legal advice on the matter. Calling Apple's support number will not shed any light on the subject, since its support personnel are not allowed to give advice related to the App Store Review Guidelines.

Submitting an app to the iOS App Store

Before you get started with submitting our application to the store, we need to review a short checklist to make sure you are ready to do so. It is a pain to reach a point in the process and realize you have something missing or haven't done something quite right. Additionally, there are a few requirements that will need to be met by a designer or the marketing team, which should not necessarily be left up to the developer.

Make sure you have done the following prior to beginning with the submission:

- Your application's `Info.plist` file is completely filled out. This includes splash screen images, app icons, app name, and other settings that need to be filled out for advanced features. Note that the app name here is what is displayed under the application icon. It can differ from the App Store name, and unlike the App Store name, it does not have to be unique from all the other apps in the store.
- You have at least three names selected for your app on the App Store. A name may be unavailable even if it is not currently taken on the App Store, as it could have been previously taken by a developer for an app that was removed from the store for some reason. You can also reserve a name ahead of time, if desired.

- You have a large 1024×1024 app-icon image. There isn't a need to include this file in the application, unless you are distributing enterprise or ad hoc builds through iTunes (the desktop application).
- You have at least one screenshot per device that your application is targeting. This includes iPhone 6 Plus, iPhone 6, iPhone 5, iPhone 4, iPad mini, iPad retina, and iPad Pro-sized screenshots for a universal iOS application. I would strongly recommend filling out all possible screenshots slots.
- You have a well-written and edited description for the App Store.
- You have selected a set of keywords to improve the search for your application.

Creating a distribution provisioning profile

Once you have double-checked the preceding checklist, we can begin the process for submission. Our first step will be to create a provisioning profile for App Store distribution.

Let's begin creating a new provisioning profile by carrying out the following steps:

1. Navigate to `https://developer.apple.com/account/`.
2. Click on **Certificates, IDs & Profiles** in the right-hand navigation bar.
3. Click on **Provisioning Profiles | All**.
4. Click on the plus button in the top-right corner of the window.
5. Select **App Store** under **Distribution** and click on **Continue**.
6. Select your app ID. You should have created one already in `Chapter 7`, *Deploying and Testing on Devices*; click on **Continue**.
7. Select the certificate for the provisioning profile. Normally, there will be only one option here. Click on **Continue**.
8. Give the profile an appropriate name, such as `MyAppAppStore`. Click on **Generate**.
9. Once complete, you can download and install the profile manually or synchronize your provisioning profiles in Xcode under **Preferences | Accounts**, as we did earlier in this book.

You will arrive at the following screen when successful:

Adding your app to iTunes Connect

For our next set of steps, we will start filling out the details of your application to be displayed on the Apple App Store.

We can begin by performing the following set of steps to set up your app in iTunes Connect:

1. Navigate to http://itunesconnect.apple.com and log in.
2. Click on **My Apps**.
3. Click the plus button in the top-left corner of the window, followed by **New App**.
4. Check **iOS** for the platform.
5. Enter an app **Name** to be displayed on the App Store.
6. Choose a **Primary Language** for your app.
7. Select your **Bundle ID**. You should have already created one in Chapter 7, *Deploying and Testing on Devices*.
8. Enter a value in the **SKU** field. This is used to identify your app in reports.
9. Click on **Continue**.
10. From here, there is a lot of required information to fill out. If you miss any, iTunes Connect is pretty helpful at displaying warnings. It should be fairly user-friendly, since the site is meant to be used by marketing professionals as well as developers.
11. Click on **Save** after making your changes.

There are a lot of optional fields, too. Make sure you fill out **Review Notes** or **Demo Account Information** if there is any additional information the app review team will require to review your application. When complete, you will see your application with the status **Prepare for Submission**, as shown in the following screenshot:

Now we need to actually upload our app to iTunes Connect. You must either upload a build from Xcode or Application Loader. Either method will produce the same results, but some prefer to use Application Loader if a non-developer is submitting the app.

Making an iOS binary for the App Store

Our final step for App Store submission is to provide our binary file containing our application to the store. We need to create the Release build of our application, signed with the distribution provisioning profile we created earlier in this chapter.

Xamarin Studio makes this very simple. We can configure the build as follows:

1. Click on the solution configuration dropdown in the top-left corner of Xamarin Studio and select **AppStore**.
2. By default, Xamarin Studio will set all the configuration options that you need to submit this build configuration.
3. Next, select your iOS application project and click on **Build | Archive for Publishing**.

After a few moments, Xamarin Studio will open the archived builds menu, which looks as follows:

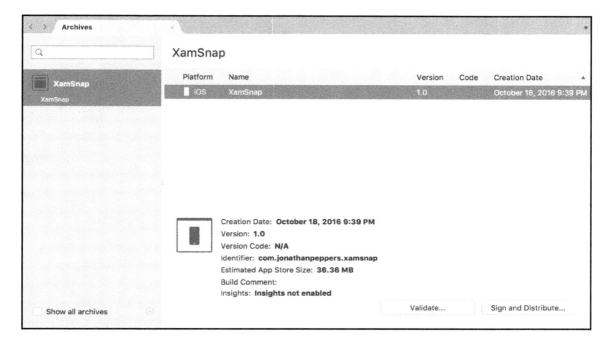

The process creates an `xarchive` file that is stored in `~/Library/Developer/Xcode/Archives`. The **Validate...** button will check your archive for any potential errors that could occur during upload, while **Sign and Distribute...** will actually submit the application to the store.

To submit your application to the store, perform the following steps:

1. Click on **Sign and Distribute...**. Don't worry, it will validate the archive before uploading.
2. Select **App Store** and click on **Next**.
3. Make sure the provisioning profile listed is for the App Store and click **Next**.
4. Review your changes and hit **Publish**.
5. Choose a location to store the `*.ipa` file and hit **Save**.
6. Click on **Open Application Loader** to move onto the upload process.

You should arrive at a screen in Xamarin Studio that looks similar to the following screenshot:

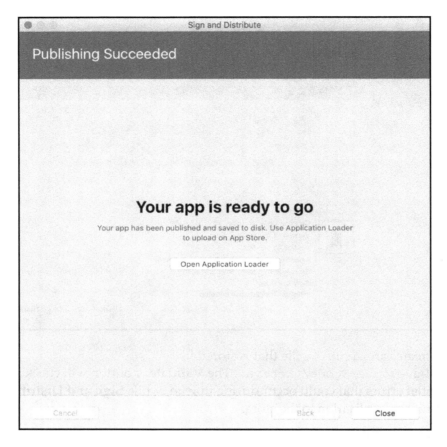

From here, using **Application Loader** is fairly straightforward:

1. Log in with your iTunes Connect credentials.
2. Select **Deliver Your App** and click on **Choose**.
3. Select the `*.ipa` file you created from Xamarin Studio and click **Open**.
4. Review the app selected for the build and hit **Next**.
5. If everything was done properly, you should see an upload progress bar followed by a success dialog.

If you return to iTunes Connect, and navigate to the **TestFlight | Test Flight Builds** tab, you will see the build you just uploaded with a status of **Processing**:

Processing ?			
Build	Upload Date	Version	Status
1.0	Nov 25, 2014	1.0	Uploaded

After a few minutes, the build will get processed and can be added to an App Store release. The next step is to select the build under the **App Store | iOS App** tab, under the **Build** section.

After hitting **Save**, you should be able to click **Submit for Review** without any remaining warnings. Next, answer the three questions about export laws, ad identifiers, and so on, and hit **Submit** as the final step to submit your app.

At this point, you have no control on the status of your application while it's waiting in line to be reviewed by an Apple employee. This can take a week or longer, depending on the current workload of apps to be reviewed and the time of year. Updates will also go through this same process, but the wait time is generally a bit shorter than a new app submission.

Luckily, there are a few situations where you can fast track this process. If you navigate to h ttps://developer.apple.com/contact/app-store/?topic=expedite, you can request for an expedited app review. Your issue must either be a critical bug fix or a time-sensitive event related to your application. Apple doesn't guarantee accepting an expedite request, but it can be a lifesaver in times of need.

Additionally, if something goes wrong with a build you submitted, you can cancel the submission by going to the top of the app details page and selecting **remove this version from review**. In situations where you discover a bug after submission, this allows you to upload a new build in its place.

Signing your Android applications

All Android packages (`apk` files) are signed by a certificate or a keystore file to enable their installation on a device. When you are debugging/developing your application, your package is automatically signed by a development key that was generated by the Android SDK. It is fine to use this debug key for development or even beta testing; however, it cannot be used on an application distributed to Google Play.

Complete the following setup to create a signed APK:

1. Click on the solution configuration dropdown in the top-left corner of Xamarin Studio and select **Release**.
2. Next, select your Android application project and click on **Build** | **Archive for Publishing**.
3. Next, select the created Android archive and click **Sign and Distribute**.
4. Choose **Ad Hoc** and click **Next**. Google Play is also an option you might look into later, but it takes a bit more time to set up (it also cannot upload the first APK for an application).
5. Select **Create a New Key**.
6. Fill out the required information for an Android keystore file and click **OK**.
7. Select the keystore file you created and click **Next**.
8. Click **Publish** and choose a location to save your APK.

Your settings for the keystore file should look similar to the following screenshot:

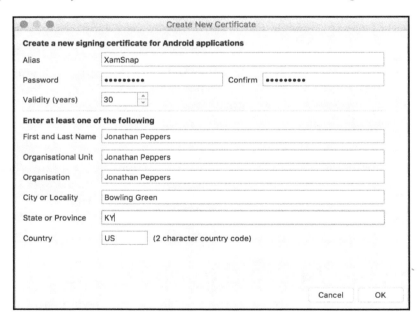

When complete, you should store your keystore file and password in a very safe place. By default, Xamarin Studio places your keys in ~/Library/Developer/Xamarin/KeyStore. Once you sign an application with this keystore file and submit it to Google Play, you will not be able to submit updates of the application without signing it with the same key. There is no mechanism to retrieve a lost keystore file. If you do happen to lose it, your only option is to remove the existing app from the store and submit a new app that contains your updated changes. This could potentially cause you to lose a lot of users.

Submitting the app to Google Play

Once you have a signed Android package, submitting your application to Google Play is relatively painless compared to iOS. Everything can be completed via the **Developer Console** tab in the browser without having to upload the package with an OS X application.

Before starting the submission, make sure you have completed the tasks on the following checklist:

- You have declared an AndroidManifest.xml file with your application name, package name, and icon declared
- You have an apk file signed with a production key
- You have selected an application name for Google Play. This is not unique across the store
- You have a 512×512 high-resolution icon image for Google Play
- You have a well-written and edited description for the store
- You have at least two screenshots. However, I recommend using all available slots, which include sizes for as well as 7 inch and 10 inch tablets

After going through the checklist, you should be fully prepared to submit your application to Google Play. The tab for adding new apps looks as follows:

To begin with, navigate to `https://play.google.com/apps/publish`and log in to your account, and carry out the following steps:

1. Select the **All Applications** tab and click on **Add new application**.
2. Enter a name to be displayed for the app on Google Play and click on **Upload APK**.
3. Click on **Upload your first APK to Production** or the **Beta** or **Alpha** channel.
4. Browse to your signed `.apk` file and click on **OK**. You will see the **APK** tab's checkmark turn green.
5. Select the **Store Listing** tab.
6. Fill out all the required fields, including **Description**, **High-res Icon**, **Categorization**, and **Privacy Policy** (or select the checkbox saying you aren't submitting a policy), and provide at least two screenshots.
7. Click on **Save**. You will see the checkmark on the **Store Listing** tab turn green.
8. Select the **Content Rating** tab and fill out the questionnaire for choosing an age-rating for your app.
9. Select the **Pricing & Distribution** tab.
10. Select a price and the countries you wish to distribute to.
11. Accept the agreement for **Content guidelines** and **US export laws**.
12. Click on **Save**. You will see the checkmark on the **Pricing & Distribution** tab turn green.
13. Select the **Ready to publish** dropdown in the top-right corner, as shown in the following screenshot, and select **Publish this app**:

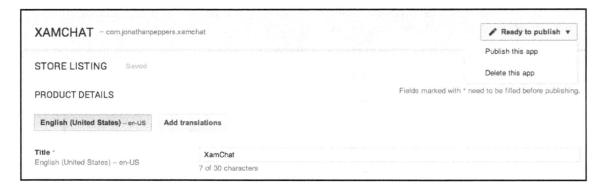

In a few hours, your application will be available on Google Play. No approval process is required, and updates to your apps are equally painless.

Google Play developer program policies

To provide a safe store environment, Google retroactively deletes applications that violate its policies and will generally ban the entire developer account–not just the application. Google's policies are aimed at improving the quality of applications available on Google Play and are not quite as lengthy as the set of rules on iOS. That being said, the following is a basic summary of Google's policies:

- Apps cannot have sexually explicit material, gratuitous violence, or hate speech.
- Apps cannot infringe upon copyrighted material.
- Apps cannot be malicious in nature, or capture private information of users without their knowledge.
- Apps cannot modify the basic functionality of users' devices (such as modifying the home screen) without their consent. If applications include features like this, it must be easy for users to turn off.
- All digital content within your application must use Google Play's in-app billing (or IAPs). Physical goods cannot be purchased with IAPs.
- Applications must not abuse cellular network usage that could result in the user incurring high bill amounts:

As with iOS, if you have a concern about one of the policies, it is best to procure professional, legal advice about the policy. For a complete list of the policies, visit `https ://play.google.com/about/developer-content-policy/`.

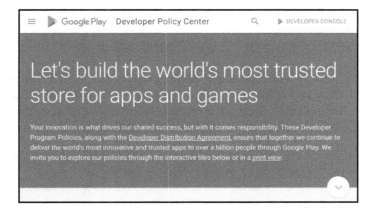

Tips for building a successful mobile app

From my personal experience, I have been submitting applications built with Xamarin to the iOS App Store and Google Play for quite some time. After delivering nearly 50 mobile applications totaling millions of downloads, a lot of lessons are learned about what makes a mobile application successful or a failure. Xamarin apps are indistinguishable from Java or Objective-C apps to the end user, so you can make your app successful by following the same patterns as standard iOS or Android applications.

There is quite a bit you can do to make your app more successful. Here are some tips to follow:

- **Pricing it right**: If your application appeals to everyone and everywhere, consider a *freemium* model that makes revenue from ad placements or IAPs. However, if your app is fairly niche, you will be much better off pricing your app at $4.99 or higher. Premium apps must hold a higher standard of quality, but can earn decent revenue on a smaller number of users.

- **Knowing your competition**: If there are other apps in the same space as yours, make sure your application is better or offers a much wider feature set than the competition. It might also be a good idea to avoid the space altogether if there are already several apps competing with yours.

- **Prompting loyal users for reviews**: It is a good idea to prompt users for a review after they open your application several times. This gives users who actively use your application a chance to write a good review.

- **Supporting your users**: Provide a valid support e-mail address or Facebook page for you to easily interact with your users. Respond to bug reports and negative reviews. Google Play even has the option to e-mail users who write reviews on your app.

- **Keeping your application small**: Staying under the 100MB limit on iOS or 50MB on Google Play will allow users to download your application on their cellular data plan. Doing this reduces the friction to install your app, as users will associate a lengthy download with a slow-running application.

- **Submitting your app to review websites**: Try to get as many reviews on the web as possible. Apple provides the ability to send coupon codes, but with the Android version of your app, you could send your actual Android package. Sending your app to review websites or popular YouTube channels can be a great way to gain free advertising.
- **Using an app analytics or tracking service**: Reporting your app's usage and crash reports can be very helpful to understand your users. Fixing crashes in the wild and modifying your user interface to improve spending behavior is very important.

There is no silver bullet to having a successful mobile application. If your application is compelling, fulfills a need, and functions quickly and properly, you could have the next hit on your hands. Being able to deliver a consistent cross-platform experience using Xamarin will also give you a head start on your competitors.

Summary

In this chapter, we covered everything you need to know to submit your application to the iOS App Store and Google Play. We covered the App Store Review Guidelines, and simplified them for the most common situations you might run into during the approval process. We went over the setup process for provisioning your app's metadata and uploading your binary to iTunes Connect. For Android, we went over how to create a production-signing key and sign your Android Package (APK) file. We went over submitting an application to Google Play, and finished the chapter with tips on delivering a successful, and hopefully profitable, application to the app stores.

I hope that with this book, you have experienced an end-to-end, practical walkthrough for developing real-world, cross-platform applications with Xamarin. C# should enable you to be very productive in comparison to the other options for mobile development. Additionally, you will save time by sharing code, without in any way limiting the native experience for your users.

Index